and confidently as the healthy DeBolt children are taught to do. Pity and despair have no place here. Instead there are humor and gaiety and guts in abundance. And what the children achieve, guided by their parents and with the all-important help of their brothers and sisters, is almost incredible. Altogether, *19 Steps Up the Mountain* is a joyful and moving story with a profound message for all parents.

Joseph P. Blank, a Roving Editor for *Reader's Digest*, is a regular contributor to that magazine. His articles have appeared in such publications as *Redbook, Harper's,* and *McCall's*, and in more than a dozen anthologies and textbooks. Mr. Blank lives in Yorktown Heights, New York.

19
STEPS
UP THE
MOUNTAIN

19 STEPS UP THE MOUNTAIN

The Story of the DeBolt Family

by JOSEPH P. BLANK

J. B. LIPPINCOTT COMPANY
Philadelphia and New York

Grateful acknowledgment is made to those who generously gave their permission to reproduce the photographs in this book.

U.S. LIBRARY OF CONGRESS CATALOGING IN PUBLICATION DATA

Blank, Joseph P
  19 steps up the mountain.

  1. Interracial adoption—United States. 2. Children, Adopted—United States. 3. Handicapped children—Family relationships. 4. DeBolt family. I. Title.
HV875.B57   362.7'34 [B]   76-22659
ISBN 0-397-01155-5

FOR NAOMI

Not a single child in this house right now was "planned." Not one was anticipated. We simply became aware of or were presented with a situation that involved the child, and we had to act on it. Sunee—she was losing her second foster home. Wendy—an American nurse wrote us from Korea that unless this battered orphan got an operation very quickly she would be blind for the rest of her life. And Karen—the only home she ever knew was a hospital, a good hospital, but still a hospital. No family. A congenital quadruple amputee. She was classified "unadoptable." J.R. was also in a hospital. He was a throwaway child, tossed back and forth between foster homes and the adoption agency. J.R. wanted a home and a family. Twe and Lee—five months ago we didn't know they existed.

Once we knew about these children, how could we turn our backs on them? Someone had to take them and love them. Someone had to give them a chance in life. We did, and we did it because we wanted to, not because we were forced to. Each one of these children has given us a "trip." Sometimes the "trip" has been kind of rough, but that's what makes the good part so very good.

A strange and lovely thing happens with each child. The moment he or she comes into this home, we can't imagine the family without that child.

—Dorothy DeBolt

We try to raise and train a child for early emancipation. We give our children love, but we are also demanding and we believe in discipline. We can be tough. We find that it pays off. The child develops into a more competent, confident, capable human being. We are not an institution for the handicapped. We don't want any child here for the rest of his or her life. We

7

want every one of these disabled children to reach a point—just as our able-bodied children do—where he or she will come to us and say, "Mom and Dad, I think I'm ready to leave the house and make it on my own."

Before a child can make such a break he must face the reality of himself and know how to deal with the reality around him. The world is not handicap-oriented. The handicapped must deal with the world of the able-bodied. They're going to have to make it and function as effective human beings in a system that is in no way geared to their crutches, braces, books, and blindness.

—Bob DeBolt

19
STEPS
UP THE
MOUNTAIN

one

I T WAS THE START of an average day in the DeBolt home in Piedmont, California. A little after seven on a July morning in 1975 Dorothy DeBolt, dressed in one of her husband's old robes, had already had breakfast. She was upstairs working at her desk in the bedroom, which doubled as an office. Deep shelves on two walls were filled with books and magazines. A second desk—Bob DeBolt's—was at an angle to hers. Nearby were four filing cabinets. There were two typewriters, two telephones, an adding machine, a telephone answering machine, a house intercom, file folders, letters—all for the purpose of bringing parents and children together through the DeBolts' agency AASK, Aid to the Adoption of Special Kids. They had created the organization to find and help families willing to adopt physically and/or mentally handicapped children, children of all races, in need of permanent homes.

At this moment Dorothy was belatedly filling out state-required adoption forms on the two children who had most recently joined the family, two girls in their early teens from Vietnam. Lee had been paralyzed by polio and had no use of her legs; Twe was blind. Each form required also that she supply information on the other members of the family. With so many, she never could be sure of accurately remembering the birth dates, so she reached into a file folder and pulled out a Xerox copy of a list for reference. It read:

THE FAMILY OF ROBERT AND DOROTHY DEBOLT

Biological Children
Mike, b. March 1948 (boy).
Mimi, b. July 1949 (girl).
Stephanie, b. January 1951 (girl).
Noël, b. December 1952 (girl).
Mary Donelle, b. July 1960 (girl).
Melanie, b. August 1960 (girl).

Other Children
Marty, Korean-Caucasian, b. September 1954 (boy). Joined family February 1957. Adopted.
Kim, Korean-Caucasian, b. February 1953 (boy). Joined family May 1959. Adopted.
Tich, Vietnamese, war-wounded paraplegic, b. December 1954 (boy). Joined family September 1969. Legal guardianship.
Anh, Vietnamese, war-wounded paraplegic, b. January 1955 (boy). Joined family September 1969. Legal guardianship.
Sunee, Korean-Caucasian, polio paralyzed, b. June 1967 (girl). Joined family September 1971. Adopted.
Dat, Vietnamese, b. August 1957 (boy). Joined family February 1972. Legal guardianship.
Trang, Vietnamese, b. September 1959 (boy). Joined family February 1972. Legal guardianship.
Karen, American black, congenital quadruple amputee, b. November 1966 (girl). Joined family October 1972. Adopted.

12

Wendy, Korean, once blind, battered child, one eye, b. March 1968 (girl). Joined family October 1973. Adopted.

Phong, Vietnamese, b. March 1965 (boy). Joined family August 1974. Legal guardianship.

John ("J.R."), American Caucasian, spina bifida paraplegic, blind, b. June 1964 (boy). Joined family November 1974. Adopted.

When she had typed out all seventeen names, with sex, age, place of birth, and state of health, she put an asterisk in front of nine of them and footnoted "Now living at home." Of the biological children, only the youngest, Melanie, was asterisked. Of the other children she marked every name but Kim, Marty, and Dat.

Outside, a brown Ford station wagon U-turned in front of the DeBolts' big Spanish mission style house on Wildwood Avenue and parked at the side of the road. Bob DeBolt, forty-five, got out of the car, his gray hair glistening with sweat. He had just jogged 2½ miles around Lake Merritt in nearby Oakland. He stepped along the path to the front porch, walking on the random-sized pink concrete blocks that were meant to resemble flagstones. Roots from the redwood and fir trees on both sides of the path had raised most of the blocks, making them an obstacle course to any stranger to the house. His children with crutches and braces found them no problem. He had been meaning to have the path replaced for a year.

He picked up the *San Francisco Chronicle* from the porch and unlocked the heavy oak door. In the spacious front hall stood a wheelchair, framed in chromium tubing and with a brown plastic back and seat. There was another wheelchair just inside the entrance to the family room–dining room.

Bob walked into the kitchen, wiped his face with the towel, and threw the towel down the chute to the basement; then he fixed himself a cup of instant coffee.

In about twenty minutes there was a clumping sound from the far end of the kitchen. The noise was made by Tich ("Tuck") and Anh ("On"), as they climbed the ten steps from their basement bedroom to the kitchen. Tich was slight in size, small-boned, sleekly muscled. Anh had the broad shoulders and heavily muscled arms of a football halfback. Both were twenty years old, and both had been injured in Vietnam early in 1968. Tich was on regular crutches that came to his armpits, while Anh had the shorter aluminum "Canadian" crutches with three-quarter circle bands just below his elbows. Both boys greeted Bob, but Tich's sharply featured face was serious while Anh grinned. Bob said, "Hi, sports."

Tich put water in the kettle on the kitchen island's built-in electric range, and Anh dropped bread into two toasters.

Suddenly Anh grimaced, leaned against a counter, and rubbed his chest.

"Bad pain, Anh?"

"Pretty bad. Pass in a minute." A nerve in Anh's right thigh still caused him frequent pain. The thigh had no other sensation, so it didn't help to rub it: instead he rubbed his chest for consolation.

Tich pulled out his wallet, asked Bob to write him a check, and counted out more than $100 in bills. "Two customers moved away and beat us out of a month's receipts. That really cuts our profit this month." Tich and Anh were partners in a daily *Oakland Tribune* paper route. They had taken it over after it had been rejected as too tough by able-bodied teenagers. The route included a four-floor and a five-floor apartment house without elevators. During the summer vacation they also worked mornings and early afternoons at Goodwill Industries in Oakland, repairing small electrical appliances.

The boys wasted little time eating. They put their cups and plates into the dishwasher and, with their rapid swing-through crutch gait, left the kitchen and went out to their car parked in the driveway.

Fifteen-year-old Trang came running up the basement steps from his bedroom. Trang was able-bodied and spent most of those summer days working as a volunteer, teaching swimming to mentally retarded children. He too had a paper route, but in the afternoon.

He told Bob, "I finished my driver ed course yesterday."

"Good. We'll go out driving a couple of times a week so you don't forget what you learned. If it slips my mind, remind me, will you?"

Trang had cold cereal and also cleared up after himself. Four people had now breakfasted and left no sign of it in the kitchen.

Bob finished his coffee and ran upstairs to shower, peeling off his sweatshirt as he went. In the bedroom he bent down and kissed the top of his wife's short blonde hair. She winked at him but went on typing. She was writing to a single man who had inquired about adopting a handicapped child. Dorothy was seven years older than Bob, but her face and slim figure belied it.

"Hi, honey," she said as she finished a sentence. "Boys get off on time?"

Bob laughed. "You always ask me that, you know? And the answer's always the same." He patted her head affectionately. "I wonder what you did when I wasn't around to ask. . . ." His voice was lost as he went into the bathroom and turned on the shower.

"I try not to think about that," Dorothy said lightly.

She looked at the clock on the table beside the bed and pulled the BASEMENT switch on the intercom. "Good morning, Phong. Time for breakfast." Then she went into the hall and called, "Girls. Good morning. Time to get up."

There were three children's bedrooms on the second floor. Melanie, nearly fifteen, Dorothy's last child by birth, had a room to herself, but she was off in New Mexico visiting Doni, Bob's daughter by his previous marriage. The second room was occupied by Twe and Lee, survivors of the Orphans Airlift plane crash outside of Saigon in early April. The last bedroom was occupied by Sunee and Karen, both eight, and seven-year-old Wendy.

Sunee and Wendy slept in twin beds. Between them on the floor was the small rectangular bed Bob had built for Karen by boxing in an infant's 4-foot mattress. Next to it was the 18-inch nightstand he had made her with a lamp attached, rewired so that it could be turned off and on by a toggle switch. It was easy for Karen to lean over and flick the switch with her arm stump.

The floor was strewn with four crutches, a pair of leg braces, and a bucketlike prosthetic device which fitted Karen's buttocks. Attached to the bucket were chocolate-colored plastic legs and braces.

Wendy got out of bed and promptly stumbled and fell over Karen's plastic legs. She often started the morning by falling over something. She stood for a moment absorbed in thought. "I can't remember where I put my glasses," she said.

"Wendy, they're right on top of your chest of drawers," said Sunee in a motherly tone.

Wendy turned, looked, laughed, and said, "I must be blind." Two years earlier she had indeed been blind. A corneal transplant at that time had given her sight in one eye.

Karen said, "That's funny, Wendy," and all three laughed.

On the first floor, in a bedroom behind the kitchen, eleven-year-old J.R. was slowly getting dressed. After wheeling himself into the adjoining bathroom to wash and brush his teeth he pushed himself to his bed from the wheelchair and slowly buttoned his shirt, pulled on trousers and socks, pushed his feet into shoes, then squirmed and pulled himself back into the wheelchair. He pressed the stem of his wristwatch. The crystal opened and he ran a finger over the hands and the raised braille dots. Then he turned on his transistor radio and listened to the news and weather report.

It was now about 9:45 and all the children had made their beds. Bob had dressed and was in the kitchen. He sautéed slices of onion, dropped two eggs into the pan, and scrambled the mixture. He ate quickly. Dorothy ran up from the basement where she had filled the washing machine with laundry—about a third of what had to be washed each day.

Bob put his arms around her waist and kissed her. "I have to get to that meeting on AASK fund raising. I hope somebody comes up with something! We're running low."

As he left Phong came up the basement steps and Wendy came running down from the second floor. The two children began setting the kitchen table.

Dorothy stood thinking for a moment. "Let's see . . . seven." She went to the pantry and removed three cans of corned beef hash.

She emptied the contents into a large skillet, half-filled another pan with water, and brought it to a boil. Counting aloud she dropped seven eggs into the water for poaching, then split English muffins and put them under the oven broiler.

By the time the food was ready, all the children had made their way to the kitchen and taken their places at the table except blind Twe, who was just arriving, moving slowly with her cautious, rolling gait and about to walk into a cupboard door that had silently opened. Sunee yelled "Stop!" and Twe froze, extended her hands, touched the door, and closed it. Then she sat down between Lee and Sunee.

Dorothy spooned hash onto seven plates and topped each portion with a poached egg. "Phong, serve the plates, please. J.R. and Wendy get the half muffins." J.R. was not yet as active as the other children, and Wendy tended to overeat and put on weight. As Phong served the others, Dorothy went upstairs to get dressed.

When she'd finished her food Wendy reached for the half-gallon of milk and began tipping the spout toward her cup. Karen said, "No, Wendy, you're not supposed to do that. You spill. Ask Phong or Sunee to do it for you."

"Yes, Wendy," chimed in Sunee. "You know you're only supposed to do it if there's a little milk in the container." With astonishingly strong hands and arms Sunee poured the milk while Wendy pursed her lips in irritation.

J.R. said, "Oh, I forgot. Phong, are you busy?"

"Why?"

"Would you get me my pills from the dining-room table?"

"Get them yourself, J.R.," Phong said in a friendly tone.

Dorothy, dressed in a blue striped shirt, light denim pants, and sneakers, just then returned to the kitchen. "J.R.," she said sharply, "you know you don't ask people to do things you can do yourself. Now get your butt into the dining room and get the pills. If you can't reach them, that's another matter. Then call somebody for help."

"Yes. Mom." J.R. wheeled himself into the next room and groped on the long dining table for a full five minutes before he came back with the bottle.

Dorothy ran down the basement steps and transferred the laundry to the dryer; next she put a load of sheets and pillow cases into the washing machine. She added soap powder scooped from a 50-pound plastic barrel. The laundry room was large. In addition to the laundry equipment it had two freezers and a second refrigerator. On one wall were shelves from floor to ceiling for canned goods. She dealt with a small wholesale grocer and bought most staples by the case.

She checked the contents of the refrigerator and returned to the kitchen as the slower eaters were finishing breakfast.

"Wendy and Phong did the dishes yesterday. So this morning—let's see—how about you, Lee, rinsing the plates and tableware and you, Sunee, putting them in the dishwasher. I'll do the pans. Karen," she added, "please sweep the floor."

Lee rolled her wheelchair parallel to the sink, then pulled herself out of the seat and perched on one arm of it. Hanging on with one hand, she rinsed the dishes with the other and handed them to Sunee. Sunee, propped on one crutch and leaning against the dishwasher door, put them in the racks. Meanwhile Karen, her eyes gleaming with determination, grasped the tall broom handle halfway down its length in her hooks and swung the bristles in awkward arcs over a muffin crumb by Twe's chair. Finally, on the fourth pass, she caught it.

Dorothy went to the kitchen bulletin board to add four items to the shopping list before she forgot them. Tacked to the board was an assortment of things: a pink and orange crayoned drawing labeled "To Mommy" and signed "Wendy"; a handmade Valentine, its paper lace curling; a recipe for eggs Florentine clipped from a newspaper; a card listing a school's holidays; a doctor's name and telephone number.

At the top of the board, carefully centered and separated from the jumble below, was a poem which had been written by Dorothy's fourth child, Noël, now away at college:

> Ye who have
> No home;
> Ye who have
> No love;
> Ye who have
> Naught;
> Unto this house
> Come
> And ye shall have.

two

WHAT DOROTHY had said that morning to Bob was true: she did not like to think of the loneliness of those six years of widowhood after her first marriage to Ted Atwood had been brought to an end by his death of a brain tumor. They had lived in Placerville then, a small town east of Sacramento, where Ted had his own insurance agency. They were so happy in their family and felt so blessed by their own children that they had adopted two more—first Marty and then Kim—out of the simple desire to share what they had with a child who had nothing. When Ted died, Dorothy took on singlehandedly the raising of seven children ranging in age from fifteen to three. She sold the agency and some of Ted's real estate investments and managed to buy the big house on Wildwood Avenue in Piedmont.

Though there were the usual problems with growing kids that all parents have, along with the terrible bouts of loneliness and constant money worries, certainly those years had not been all bad. Child-rearing problems were balanced by plenty of satisfactions and just pure fun, and there had been exciting times too, as when Dorothy, who had joined Parents Without Partners for some adult companionship, was named U.S. Single Parent of the Year for 1968–1969. And, then, only a short time before she and Bob met on the blind date that led to their marriage seven months later, she had added Tich and Anh to the family.

Seeing Sunee come into the kitchen on that particular July morning in 1975, she wondered if the child would have mastered the big curving staircase from the front hall *yet* if it hadn't been for Tich and Anh.

Sunee was the first child Dorothy and Bob adopted together, in a way almost a wedding present, for they first learned of her shortly after returning from their honeymoon in June 1970.

It began with a telephone call from a Mrs. Pedro Castillo, who knew of Dorothy's interest in homeless, handicapped children. The Castillos had several adopted children of their own, and had taken on temporarily a three-year-old Korean-American girl. The child, then known as Sun Hee, was paralyzed from the waist down, the victim of polio at age ten months. Her Korean mother had been married to an American, had followed him to this country, and had been abandoned. She had returned to Korea with her newborn daughter, but the social ostracism there caused by mixed parentage, plus the lack of means of providing for Sun Hee's medical care, had caused her to place Sun Hee in an orphanage when the child was twenty months old. There the executive director of the Holt Adoption Program met the mother and resolved to rescue the child. Sun Hee was brought back to the States and placed temporarily with the Castillos, since Mrs. Castillo was a member of the Holt adoption board.

It was clear that Sun Hee would need braces and crutches for the rest of her life for short distances, and very likely a wheelchair for longer distances. When she was fifteen, she might have a spinal fusion but until then would wear a trunk jacket. Sun Hee needed to be carried several times a day, and Mrs. Castillo had a serious back problem. The Holt agency could not find a family that would take her. Could Dorothy help? The child, Mrs. Castillo assured her, was delightful.

Dorothy and Bob had talked about adopting a child and expected to do so, but not quite so soon after their marriage. Dorothy made some telephone calls, but could find no one willing to adopt a child with Sun Hee's physical problems. Six weeks later Mrs. Castillo telephoned to report that the child had been placed with a couple who planned to adopt her. But months after that, when Sun Hee was nearly four years old, Mrs. Castillo called Dorothy again to report the adoption plans had been canceled. The prospective father had changed his mind, and his wife felt it best not to try to persuade him to keep the child.

"Sun Hee must be having a rough time," Mrs Castillo said. "She's very intelligent. Aware. She was given up by her own mother. Now she's being pushed out of her second home in the States. The Holt people can't find a family that'll take her."

"Let me think about it and call you tomorrow," Dorothy said.

That night she described Sun Hee's predicament to Bob. "That kid needs a permanent home. She can't keep being kicked around. You know what kind of damage that'll do."

Bob was silent for a long moment, then, "Call her back and tell her Sun Hee has a home," he said.

"Do you mean that?"

"Sure. Haven't we been talking about adopting?"

"Of course, but our first idea was an older child, somebody Melanie's age." Dorothy's youngest daughter was eleven.

"What's the difference? This kid needs a home. Needs love. Needs to feel wanted. It's all here, just waiting for her."

Dorothy quickly rose from her chair, kissed her husband, said, "I'm crazy about you," and made the call.

Mrs. Castillo said, "You're the right family for this child."

"Sure," Dorothy said. "We've had experience with paralyzed kids. Sun Hee's problems don't worry us. Sometimes I think that handicapped kids are easier to raise than able-bodied ones. They aren't confused about who they are and what they are. I've told you about Tich and Anh. They'll be good therapists for Sun Hee. They know what crutches and braces are all about. Why don't you talk to Sun Hee's caseworker and get this thing rolling?"

"That's a little awkward," Mrs. Castillo replied. "I'm not supposed to get involved in placement. That's the job of Sun Hee's caseworker. And you know how touchy social workers can be about their authority."

"You're right. Tell you what. I'll contact the Holt people and tell them I want to adopt a young, disabled Korean girl. I'll tell them that I heard about Sun Hee's availability and ask them to suggest us to her caseworker. If Holt is having trouble placing Sun Hee I'd think that cooperation will be no problem."

The caseworker telephoned to make an appointment, and Dorothy briefed Bob for the visit. "Be nice,"

24

she told him. "There will be all kinds of questions that you may feel are asinine, but don't lose your cool."

Dorothy had been through dozens of such interviews, beginning with Marty's adoption years ago, and they never failed to exasperate her. "How many children do you have? . . . Why do you want another disabled child? . . . Are you sure this is what you want to do? . . . What are your feelings about handicapped children? . . . Might not this adoption affect your other children adversely? . . . Would it not deny the other children the attention they deserve? . . . If there is an inheritance, another child will reduce the shares of the others. . . . I will have to ask each of your children how they feel about your wanting to adopt a child and I'll have to point out to them this inheritance matter. . . ."

Next the social worker brought Sun Hee for a short visit. Dorothy and Bob were immediately charmed by this lovely child with the almond-shaped lids, long lashes, silken dark hair, and alert, brown eyes flecked with gold.

After she left, they read in each other's eyes the same message: "This little girl is for us."

It took two more visits, and a third when Sun Hee was left alone with the family for part of a day, for the DeBolts to be approved. They got a letter from the young mother who had originally hoped to adopt the child. It described Sun Hee's warm, outgoing personality, the playthings she liked, the things she could do for herself, her intelligence, her awareness, her sensitivity to others. It was a letter of love, and it was followed by several telephone calls. "I'm preparing Sun Hee for the change of families," the woman explained. "I told her that we loved her very much and we wanted to do what was best for her. We told her that it would be wonderful to live with a big family where she had many brothers and sisters. We told her that she would really enjoy everybody in it. I'll bring her and all her things to you on Friday."

Sun Hee's biological mother, too, had written a letter from Korea addressed to whoever would adopt her:

I am the natural mother of Sun Hee. But from now on you will be the mother of her. . . . It will take a little time to get aquainted with her. But she is very cute and friendly and so she will get aquainted with all of you very soon. As for the food, she eats pretty well. There is a great difference between our food and the one of yours. And so it will also take some time for her to get used to the american food. She likes the beef very much. She likes the boiled beef and rice. You can mix the rice and beef soup. The boiled rice is better. . . . She enjoys the milk and chocolate very much. She doesn't eat the chicken and pork. She likes almost all the fruit. Sun Hee used to sleep with her grand-mom and so she will have some difficulties with bed. I think you had better sleep with her for the time being. I have so many words to tell you that I can't arrange them all on the paper. . . . I want you to write to me and then I can give you more information in my letter. At this writing I come to feel something wet in my eyes. But I know that I must pray for her happiness. . . .

The child had been loved by two mothers already.

In mid-September, 1971, the young mother who was relinquishing Sun Hee drove the child to the De-Bolt home. The child was quiet. Neither Dorothy nor the other children pushed conversation. Eleven-year-old Melanie showed her the family room with the two old steamer trunks filled with toys, games, books, hats, and scarves. Sun Hee curiously opened a picture book and tried on a hat.

26

The young mother asked to see the child's room and carried the suitcase to it. "Sun Hee will share this room with Melanie," Dorothy said. "This is her bed and her chest of drawers and she has plenty of closet space. Why don't I put away her clothes?"

"Please, let me," the mother said. "I can put her things in the same drawers as they were in the bureau at home. That way she'll know where everything is." She slowly filled the drawers, lingering on each article.

Downstairs, she chatted for a while with Dorothy and the other children. She tried to be casual, but Dorothy saw how shaken she was. She managed to say good-bye lightly, while Dorothy assured Sun Hee that it would be easy to visit her former home.

During the first weeks Sunee—the DeBolts had decided it was easier to drop the *h*—frequently moaned and whimpered in her sleep. It took months for her to adjust to the change in parents. At first she always referred to the previous couple as "my other mommy and daddy." Then, as memories of the old parent-child relationship dimmed the previous couple became "Cindy's mommy and daddy," and Dorothy and Bob were established as "Mommy and Daddy."

Sunee had brought with her a panicky fear of being in a closed or dark room alone. So one day Dorothy sat on the edge of Sunee's bed and said, "Sunee, I'm going out of the room and I'm going to close the door. I'll be right outside the door. Then, in a few minutes, I'll come back in here. While I'm outside, you won't be alone."

"Who's going to be here with me?" she said fearfully.

"God will be with you. He's always with you."

"How does He do that?"

"He's always with anyone who believes in Him."

Dorothy rose and left the bedroom, closing the door behind her.

Sunee immediately began screaming in terror.

"I'm right here, honey," Dorothy called. "Right here. But you're not alone."

"Open the door!" Sunee yelled. "Open the door!"

"I'll leave it closed. For just a minute."

Sunee hobbled to the door and tried to open it. After a few seconds Dorothy said, "All right, Sunee," and let her pull the door open. But in the bedroom, Dorothy said, "You don't believe what I told you about God."

"I want to believe it, but I don't believe it," Sunee admitted.

"All right, honey, I'll sit here with you for a while." After a few minutes Dorothy said, "Let's try it the other way around. I'll stay in the room alone, and you go out in the hall and close the door. I'm not going to worry about a thing because I know God is here."

After Sunee closed the door, Dorothy called, "Sunee, you're out there all alone and the door is closed. Are you afraid?"

"No."

"Why not? What's the difference if you're on that side of the closed door or this side of the closed door?"

"This isn't my room."

"But it really is just like a room. You're alone and the door is closed."

Sunee couldn't work that out to her satisfaction.

Over the next weeks Dorothy and Sunee talked about her being alone behind a closed door. Finally Sunee willingly agreed to let Dorothy stand on the outside of the closed door for a minute. Then it became several minutes. Once Dorothy went down the hall to her bedroom, then returned. She opened Sunee's door and announced, "I wasn't even outside the door, Sunee, and you weren't even scared."

"I thought you were out there."

"Well, I wasn't and you weren't scared. It didn't really matter whether or not I was out there."

After conquering her panic at the closed door, Sunee took up the struggle against her fear of the dark. Dorothy sat with her in the darkened bedroom talking easily and lightly. After several evenings Dorothy said, "Can you feel me?"

"Sure, Mommy." She reached out and touched Dorothy's arm.

"Okay. Now I'm going to get up and just stand a few feet away. All right. Reach out and try to touch me."

"I can't reach you."

"But you know I'm here and you're not afraid, are you?"

"No, I'm not."

Eventually Dorothy left the unlighted room and closed the door. During the first few attempts Sunee was near hysteria, but after many more tries she gradually became convinced that nothing terrible was going to happen to her.

With all her fears, Sunee was lovable and loving, and Dorothy was overjoyed to have her. Much of her pleasure came from seeing Sunee's impact on the family. Melanie willingly carried her up and down the stairs, brushed her hair, and played with her. Eighteen-year-old Noël took her for drives in the car and showed her off to friends. Bob dressed and undressed her, bathed her, played with her, and read her stories.

Within a few days, whenever Bob appeared, Sunee would grin and her eyes would shine when she said, *"There's* my new daddy." Bob was ecstatic. Tich and Anh complained—but good-naturedly—that they were not getting equal time with the new sister.

A few weeks after Sunee's arrival Dorothy took her shopping at the Piedmont Grocery Store. Sunee was wearing her braces, but Dorothy carried her into the market and slipped her into a shopping cart. On the way down an aisle she encountered a woman who lived a few blocks from the DeBolt house. The woman asked, "Is this the new one I've heard about?"

Dorothy introduced Sunee, and the woman said, "My, you do have a houseful now."

"Yes, and Sunee is a wonderful child. We're so glad she's part of the family."

"I'm sure it's all very lovely," the woman said, "but don't you think it would be wiser to discourage perpetuation of the inferior?" She glanced down at the child's paralyzed limbs.

Dorothy was shocked. She looked down and was relieved to see that Sunee showed no comprehension. In this instance words came to Dorothy when she needed them. She snapped, "Right—and don't *you* forget to take your birth control pills." She wheeled away the cart so fast that Sunee turned and gave her a startled look.

Sunee had an innocence about her disability that the family found startling. She knew she was different, but she had not yet learned that her difference was a disadvantage. Once Dorothy took her to the local school playground and they sat on a bench, watching children on the swings and seesaws. Suddenly Sunee asked, "If those children are good, will they get braces and crutches?"

"You sure have a wonderfully cockeyed view of life," Dorothy said, laughing. "No, they won't get crutches and braces. They can get around without them."

Just then a boy approached and said, "What's wrong with her legs?"

"She's had polio," Dorothy said.

"What's polio?" he asked.

Dorothy suddenly realized than an entire generation of Americans was growing up without any knowledge of polio. It was as unfamiliar to them as the bubonic plague. How different from the days when she was first a mother!

Sunee would playfully mock her father's interest in her progress. When he arrived home one evening, she greeted him with his own usual first question: "Hello, sweetheart. Did you have a good day?"

"Yes, I did." He grinned in response.

"Sweetheart, show me how well you walk today."

Bob demonstrated his walk.

"Why can't you walk like I do with both feet together?" Sunee asked.

"I never learned to walk that way."

"That's all right, Daddy. You be good, and someday I'll teach you."

When Sunee first joined the family she had very little skill with her braces and crutches. She would advance the crutches about 3 inches, then drag her shoes toward them, slightly raise the crutches again for another small advance, and follow that with more shoe dragging. The ¾-inch-high rug in the foyer represented an insurmountable obstacle. Her shoes caught on the edge of it, and she was blocked. She moved faster without crutches, crawling along the floor on hands and elbows.

Dorothy and Bob didn't want to make a point of her learning proper crutch technique until she felt comfortable with the family. Meanwhile, she had the examples of Tich and Anh always before her, could see how they moved quickly and nimbly across the floor in a swing-through gait and how they maneuvered up and down stairs.

In about a week after Sunee's arrival Dorothy noticed her staring at the circular staircase in the front hall, especially when Tich or Anh climbed it to go to what was then their bedroom on the second floor. It was impossible for her to emulate their braces-and-crutches climb; she could barely drag herself from one room to another on her crutches. Yet she kept looking at the staircase. The nineteen steps were a mountain.

One Saturday morning she went over to the staircase, turned, dropped her crutches, and let herself fall into a sitting position on the first step. Then she turned, facing up the staircase. She tried to claw and wriggle herself up the 8-inch riser to the second step but couldn't make it. After pausing to catch her breath an idea occurred to her. She shifted over to the railing. Again facing up the stairs, she stretched her arm to grasp the farthest wrought-iron baluster within reach of her left hand and put the palm of her right hand on the second step. Pulling with her left hand and pushing with her right palm she wrenched herself onto the second step. She turned to the sitting position and lifted her useless braced legs to the step. She placed her crutches two steps above her.

Then she twisted, again grabbed the farthest baluster with her left hand, placed her right palm on the third step, and heaved herself onto it. Again she flipped her legs and placed the crutches on a higher step.

She repeated the grim, exhausting procedure for each step, saying not a word during the entire climb. She grunted, panted, and sweated her way up. Midway up the staircase, she was spent, but after a few minutes' rest she resumed her climb at a slower pace.

Bob was standing at the back of the second floor landing. After a time he couldn't bear watching her struggle and he went into the bedroom. When he returned to the landing some time later, she was still climbing.

It took almost forty minutes, but Sunee scaled those nineteen steps. Bob knelt beside her on the landing as she lay there, sweating and gasping for breath. He held her and smoothed back her hair, too shaken to say anything. His pride in her was beyond expression. He felt blessed that she was his child. She smiled up at him, and her eyes shone with triumph.

Then Bob decided that she was ready for more triumphs, and talked with Tich and Anh about it. "Sunee needs your help. Mom and I can't teach her the swing-through gait or how to handle the staircase. Only you can." Bob saw a light smile play at the corners of Tich's mouth; he seemed to try to stand straighter on his crutches.

Anh said, "Don't know, Bob. She pretty young kid. We try."

"We do it," said Tich.

33

After discussion the boys concluded that Sunee had to maneuver the stairs in an upright position. Crawling took too much time and effort.

On the first morning of the Christmas school holiday sixteen-year-old Tich motioned four-year-old Sunee toward the foot of the stairs. He was all business. She was all apprehension. "You learn climb stairs," Tich announced. "No big deal. You listen. You watch. Okay. Now, put left hand on railing like this and reach under with fingers and grab this thing"—the baluster. "Get good grip. Hang one crutch on right shoulder like this. Now put right crutch on step. Now you pull with left hand on railing and push up with right arm on crutch. See? I go right on to step."

Sunee tried it. The pull-push action required both technique and strength. She was carrying the additional burden of one-fourth of her own weight in braces and corset. "I can't do it," she cried. "It's too hard."

"We try again tomorrow," Tich said.

Occasionally Dorothy or Bob watched the lessons, standing in the entrance to the kitchen or sitting in a chair in the front hall. Neither ever said a word, and usually both pupil and teacher were oblivious to their presence.

After five or six attempts Sunee still couldn't mount that first step. Tich said, "Okay, Sunee, what's the matter?"

"I can't do it."

"Why you can't?"

She was silent.

"Why?"

"I'm afraid."

"Of what?"

"Falling."

"You no be afraid. I right behind you."

When several more sessions passed without any progress, Tich changed his approach. "You don't try hard enough," he admonished.

"I do. I just can't get up there."

Tich's voice hardened and he leaned toward Sunee's face, saying, "Don't tell me you can't! I have crutches and braces same as you." He slapped his knuckles against her lower abdomen, producing a dull thump on her plastic corset. He rapped the front of his corset. "See? Just the same. I don't wanna hear you can't do it. Don't wanna hear it! Now you do it! You do what I do. You do it right now!"

Sunee obediently turned to the step. Pulling and pushing, straining and grunting, she heaved herself to the first step. She turned her head to Tich; tears were running down her cheeks. "There!" she yelled angrily.

Bob quietly rose from his chair and slipped back into the kitchen. Tears were on his cheeks also.

Later Tich told Bob, "Sunee make that first step."

"Great. Took some doing, huh?"

"Not too much."

Each day she practiced the steps. It was slow, exhausting work. It took a week for her to climb three steps. Tich coached her along, and Anh stood behind her most of the time to break her fall if she lost her balance and toppled backward. Then her determination eliminated fear, and she told Anh that he didn't have to protect her. Dorothy was cooking one day when she heard a crash in the front hall. She ran in and saw Sunee sprawled across the bottom step of the staircase. "I'm all right, Mommy," Sunee assured her. She checked to see that her leg braces were locked in the straight position (leg braces are hinged at the knees to allow a sitting position), grabbed the baluster and pulled herself upright. Her face was set. She began her climb again. On reaching the fifth step she raised a crutch and beat the step several times in anger. Then she looked at Dorothy and said, "Tomorrow that step won't make me fall."

About three months after her arrival Anh knocked on the door of Dorothy's bedroom and said, "Mom, we wanna show you very important thing. Sunee has surprise for you."

Dorothy went to the second floor landing. Tich and Sunee stood at the bottom of the staircase. Sunee began struggling up the stairs. Sometimes she lost her grip on the banister, but she didn't fall. After the exertion of climbing four or five steps, she stopped to catch her breath. But she hoisted and heaved and willed herself up those nineteen steps. It took her twenty-five minutes. When she reached the second floor landing, Dorothy grabbed her and hugged her and exclaimed, "I'm so proud of you. So proud."

"Then why are you crying, Mommy?" Sunee panted.

"They're happy tears, Sunee."

Sunee licked her cheek and said, "Yes, they taste happy."

Then Dorothy hugged Tich and Anh. They were grinning, bursting with a sense of achievement. Dorothy stepped back from them and said, "You guys are something else."

While Sunee was acquiring skill on the stairs the boys were teaching her their swing-through method of walking as well: how to place the crutch tips 12 to 18 inches ahead of her, push forward with her shoulders and at the same time lift herself off the floor, then swing her legs in an arc, so that her feet landed ahead of the crutch tips. In their uninterrupted, flowing motion, they thrust forward their upper torsos, advanced their crutch tips again, and swung between the crutches.

For the young novice, the gait was frightening. During the moment of the swing she was flying, not sure where or how she would land. Sunee kept saying "I'll fall, I'll fall."

Anh told her, "Come on. You learn it. You gotta. Now take you all day to get through the house. How you gonna go to school dragging your feet? No way. So come on."

The boys began Sunee with a 2-inch swing-through, then 4, 6, 8, 10. Each few inches of progress brought her lavish praise and their own form of bribery. "You swing this far," Tich told her, spreading his hands about 18 inches, "and I show you a trick."

When Sunee met the challenge, Tich said, "Here's a trick." He dropped a sheet of paper on the floor: "Now pick up without sitting on floor."

Sunee tried extending the crutches until her body was at an angle and reached down with one hand. It didn't work.

"Watch," instructed Tich. With the rubber tip of his left crutch he shoved the paper to a wall. He then slid it up the wall with the tip. Shortening his grip on the horizontal crutch, he reached over and plucked the sheet from the wall with his right hand. He winked at Sunee and she winked back in appreciation.

While teaching her the swing-through gait, they also showed the child how to fall without hurting herself. Knowing how to hit the floor reduced her fear of taking a big arc on the swing-through. The trick was in learning to get rid of her crutches: the tendency in falling is to hang on to them, which can cause a fractured arm or broken nose. So Tich and Anh fell dozens of times for Sunee, showing her how to drop the crutches aside and take the impact on her palms, with arms slightly bent at the elbows for a spring-action effect. They trained her on pillows, first catching her before she hit, then encouraging her to take the fall on her own. By the time she had done her first practice fall on the bare floor, she had complete confidence in herself.

Rising from the floor took longer to learn. She had to place her crutches upright, then climb them like a person going up a rope hand over hand without use of legs. Sunee had to pull not only her body weight but the weight of her braces and corset. Bob and the boys put her on a regimen of pushups to strengthen her arms and shoulders. During the first several weeks she toppled over, bruising her elbows, cutting a lip, and raising bumps on her cheeks. Still, she disliked asking others to help her to her feet. "I'll get up by myself soon," she assured Anh. "I'm tired of hurting myself."

One day she was playing alone on the floor of the family room. Dorothy was cooking in the kitchen and, after a time, waited to hear the crash of braces as Sunee tried to stand.

There was no such sound, so she glanced into the family room. Sunee was erect on her crutches. "Well, great!" her mother exclaimed. "How did you do that?"

Sunee enunciated her reply slowly and deliberately: "*Care*–ful–ly."

three

THOSE GUYS certainly were "something else," and no one knew it better than Dorothy. Before joining her and her seven children when she was still a widow late in the summer of 1969, Tich and Anh had come a long way from near death in a hospital in Da Nang. Both had been permanently crippled by shrapnel, and both had been losing the fight against various infections, when they were discovered by a member of an organization called the Committee of Responsibility (COR), a group of American doctors and laymen working to bring young war victims to the States for treatment unavailable in Vietnam.

Dorothy had been in touch with COR, and she had originally offered to try to find foster homes for three paraplegic fourteen-year-old boys, Tich, Anh, and another named Minh. All three were in Stanford Convalescent Hospital after eight months of surgery and treatment at Mt. Zion Hospital in San Francisco. At Stanford they were being given physical therapy and tutoring. The plan was for them to complete their rehabilitation in an American home before returning to Vietnam.

Dorothy hadn't been able to find anyone to take even one of the three boys, despite the fact that COR would pay all medical expenses during their stay. She discussed the situation with her children, and in the end they offered to take two of the three boys themselves. Since Tich and Anh had the closest bond, it was they who came.

The children were eager to have them. Noël, who at sixteen had finally gotten a bedroom to herself only a few months earlier, willingly offered it and helped to get it ready. Stephanie, nineteen, had plans to move into an apartment for her first semester at college, but she postponed her move so she could be at home to help out.

Dorothy had had no experience with paraplegics, and her education began at the hospital before she brought Tich and Anh home. The boys were incontinent: they had no control over their bowels, and each wore a urine bag strapped to the inside of the thigh and connected by a tube to the penis. The bag had to be cleaned daily, and they knew how to take care of this themselves. Dorothy would have to watch for fever, chills, headaches—any signs of possible urinary tract infections. She was to remind them of their four kinds of pills to be taken every day, and once a week she should bring them to the hospital for urine and stool analyses. She was to make sure they did pushups and exercises with weights to strengthen their arms and shoulders; and she must check frequently for pressure sores, especially on the buttocks—and especially on Tich, who was prone to them. Tich also had an infection on his penis which he must remember to treat with an ointment supplied by the hospital.

The bedroom that Noël had given up was on the

first floor; the two boys were not very expert yet at getting around. Of the two, Anh was the most proficient; he could walk fairly well and he could manage two or three low steps, but that was all.

The night after she brought them home, along with their collapsible wheelchairs, crutches, and possessions, Dorothy knocked on their bedroom door as they were preparing to go to bed. Inside it was all freshly painted, with new curtains and a sign on the wall saying "WELCOME, BROTHERS."

"Boys," she began uncertainly, "we're all a family now, but in a way you and I are going to be like patients and nurse. I want to learn how your braces work and check you for pressure sores."

"Pressure sores very bad," Anh said. "Bad infection. Long, long time to heal."

The boys removed their clothes and Dorothy nearly gasped. Their thighs were hardly larger than a baseball bat. Tich had virtually no buttocks—just skin covering bone. Scars from innumerable skin grafts marked his back all the way down to his heels.

Dorothy said, "Oh, boy—this scar on your left leg looks just like a sunflower. Know what a sunflower is?"

Tich said no, and during the time it took to describe one she recovered her composure.

Then she asked him about the raw spot on his buttock, and he explained he had pressure sores from sitting too much in one position—or from where the brace pressed the skin.

"Why is your left leg out stiff like that?"

"Can't bend leg. In Vietnam hospitals too long. Maybe one year, just stay in bed. Knee get stiff, become like bone." The calcified knee was the size of a grapefruit.

Just then Anh groaned, doubled over, and grabbed his left thigh. "Anh, what is it? What can I do? Tell me!"

Anh took a deep breath and forced a smile. "It's okay. Okay. Nerve in leg. Make pain many times a day. Doctor say can do nothing. You no worry."

Anh's body was actually in better shape than Tich's. Tich had been nearly cut in half by artillery fire while he was swimming in a canal. Anh had stepped on a land mine which had exploded pieces of shrapnel all over him up to his face, but the only major damage had been to his spinal cord. He had good skin tissue, better blood flow, and some feeling in the thigh of one of his legs. It was that feeling which was now causing him pain.

Fighting tears, Dorothy picked up Tich's braces. "Wow! These are heavy."

"Maybe twenty, twenty-five pounds," Tich said. "Anh brace not so heavy."

Tich's leg braces, running from the soles of his feet to his pelvis, were attached to a corset made of metal, leather, and foam rubber padding which extended half-way up his rib cage. The padding had dark spots of blood from chafing and pressure. Because Tich's left leg tended to dislocate at the hip, the hospital brace maker had built the left brace stronger, and therefore heavier, than the right. Tich himself weighed no more than 80 pounds, so he carried a lifetime burden of nearly a third of his own weight.

"Well, boys," she said, "I think I've had enough education for one day. Anything you need? Okay. Don't forget your medications. And, Tich, you're supposed to apply that ointment." She kissed them. "Good night. I'm glad you're in our family." She paused. "If you want to, you can call me Mom. I'd like that."

The next morning Anh hobbled quickly into the kitchen where Dorothy was making breakfast. "Mom, Tich and me need condoms."

"What!"

"Condoms. Hospital forget to put in bag."

"What for?"

"Condom taped to penis. Attached to tube. Tube attached to urine bag."

"Oh. All right. I didn't know that thing was a condom."

"Right away, Mom. Acid make condom break."

"Yes. All right. Any special kind?"

"I think Trojans. With little tip at end."

"How many?"

"A lot."

Dorothy called the druggist, an elderly man whom she had once heard refer to her as "that nice widow lady with all the children." She told him she needed to order some condoms.

There was a pause. Then: "Condoms, Mrs. Atwood?"

"Yes, about three dozen Trojans, please."

Pause. "Did you say three dozen?"

"Yes."

"Uh . . . yes, well . . . Noon delivery all right?"

"No, you'd better send them as soon as possible."

She hung up and laughed aloud as she imagined him telling his clerks about "that wild widow who lives on Wildwood." Hearing her laughter, the boys looked puzzled, but she decided not to explain.

Although occasionally the tube became detached

from the urine bag, these accidents were not nearly so embarrassing for Tich and Anh as their inability to control their bowels and their tendency toward diarrhea. After a few incidents, Dorothy and they agreed on the use of diapers. Eventually their bodies would learn to release wastes at regular forty-eight-hour intervals. Meanwhile Dorothy cleaned and disinfected diapers daily.

She also spent at least two hours a day cleaning and soaking Tich's persistent pressure sore. A dozen times a week she lifted Tich into the station wagon (Anh could make it on his own), loaded two wheelchairs into the back, and made trips to the hospital, doctors, brace maker, and went on other errands incidental to their lives. She did the same lifting and loading twice every morning, to take the boys to and from school. Tich and Anh had been immediately enrolled in the Piedmont Junior-Senior High School, where they had a half-day schedule and their classes all on the ground floor. Though there was a school for orthopedically handicapped children in Oakland, Dorothy thought they should start right off learning to function in an unhandicapped world.

During the first two months, Dorothy was constantly apprehensive about infection and falls. She had to keep reminding the boys to take their pills, and whenever she heard the crash of crutches, braces, and body, she'd run to it in fear of broken limbs. But then she realized that these anxieties were of no value to them or to her. She said, "Look, I don't mind carrying you up and down stairs and getting you in and out of the bathtub, but the pills you can do yourselves. Unless you want to get a bad infection and go back to the hospital, take them." And when she heard them fall, she ignored it. The boys had shown her they knew perfectly well how to fall safely—how to flip aside the crutches as they went down and take the impact on their outstretched palms. Usually this worked, though one time Anh bruised his shoulder and cheekbone, and Tich once cut his forehead badly enough that she had to take him to the hospital to have the wound stitched.

Dorothy was learning all the time. But there was one discovery she didn't welcome, and it came from the world outside the house. She was approached one night by a woman at a political gathering who said: "You're Dorothy Atwood. Do you know what I think of you and those two Vietnamese? I think you're a traitor to your country!" The woman stalked away, leaving Dorothy astonished and confused. What did she mean? There seemed to be no explanation for the attack, until Dorothy remembered that the Committee of Responsibility was identified with opposition to American participation in the Vietnamese war and was considered by many hawks in the Bay Area to be a left-wing organization.

There was another incident soon after. A female reporter telephoned about a speech Dorothy was scheduled to make on behalf of the Committee. She asked if Tich and Anh came from villages associated with the Viet Cong or with Saigon.

"I really don't know," Dorothy said. "But I could try to check it out for you."

"I would have thought that you'd have checked that out before taking them in."

"What's the difference?" Dorothy asked.

The reporter was indignant. "If they're North

45

Vietnamese sympathizers then the Communists should be taking care of them. They certainly shouldn't have been brought to this country."

Dorothy was momentarily taken aback. Then she yelled, "They're children! Don't you understand? Children! I don't care if they're Ho Chi Minh's grandchildren. They're kids! They've been terribly hurt through no fault of their own. They've suffered. They need care, and people to care about them. They need help!" She banged the phone into the cradle.

Before he'd left the hospital to live with the Atwoods, Tich had been fitted with new braces and torso corset. He soon complained about them, and Dorothy told him, "Give them a chance, Tich. Maybe you just have to get used to them."

"Brace no good," he insisted.

Then, when he was trying to get from his chair to the bed one night, his left leg dislocated. "Mom," he called, "please you come."

The sight of the dislocation turned her stomach. "I'll call the doctor," she said.

"No doctor. You do."

"I'll hurt you."

"No hurt. No feeling. Remember? You push back. Real hard. Happen many time in hospital. New brace supposed to fix."

She gingerly picked up the leg. It was light, flaccid, lifeless, like the leg of a big rag doll. She felt with the thighbone for hip socket, found it, and gently pushed.

"Hard, Mom, hard."

She shoved, and the bone slipped into the socket.

"Brace no good."

"Well, give it another few days." She felt shaky. She went into the kitchen, mixed a martini, and took a big gulp.

She listened to Tich's complaints for three more days, then called the orthopedic surgeon recommended by COR. He told her to take Tich to Matt Lawrence, a brace maker in Oakland. Lawrence, who wore a brace himself as the result of childhood polio, made some adjustments, then told her, "See how this works. If the thigh dislocates, get him out of the brace and into the wheelchair and bring the brace back to me."

Once again the leg popped out, and Tich was confined to the wheelchair, which he hated, while Lawrence tried to alter the brace to prevent dislocation. He couldn't seem to devise an effective design; Dorothy had to return to him with Tich five times.

After yet another unsuccessful visit to Lawrence, Tich complained bitterly on the way home. "Brace never going to work. He not do it right. Why this happen to me? Nothing go right. Brace no good. Sore no heal. Maybe have to go to hospital for skin graft. . . ."

She made a decision. After parking the car in front of the house she turned to him and looked him straight in the eyes. "Who in hell do you think you are, complaining and moaning, while Matt Lawrence and his people are knocking themselves out trying to build a brace that will work right? Those people are breaking their necks to help and all you do is let yourself drown in self-pity. What do you have to complain about?" She almost choked on her harsh words, and she paused for breath. "So you've got a couple of legs that don't work. What about the kids who've had their brains damaged? What about the kids who are blind? What about the kids who can't hear and talk? What about the kids who are paralyzed from the neck down? And you complain!" The tears came to Tich's eyes. "I'm disgusted with you," she finished.

She picked him up, carried him into the house, plunked him in a large chair in the front hall, and stormed upstairs to her bedroom. She banged the door shut, then stood against it breathing heavily. "Oh, God, please forgive me," she whispered. "Please understand why I did it. Please make what I did help Tich." She she went into the bathroom and vomited.

That evening they exchanged very few words. The next day Tich told her, "I sorry I think only of myself. I sorry I not think about anybody else."

"I know," Dorothy answered. "We don't have to say anything more about it."

A short time later Dorothy was dashing around the house in preparation for a luncheon appointment when she glanced out the window and saw low-hanging, gray clouds. "Dear God, don't let it rain today," she said aloud. "Please."

Tich was nearby in his chair. He had been silent, but now he looked up and asked, "You talk to God, Ma?"

"Yes, Tich, all the time."

"Maybe you do me favor."

"Sure. What?"

"You ask Him make me walk again, Ma?"

That time she couldn't stop herself. She started to cry and went running out of the room. Tich came rushing after her in his wheelchair. He caught up with her in the kitchen, patted her arm comfortingly, said, "Ma, you no cry. I can no walk. I can do many things."

She turned to him and managed a smile. "Tich,

God may not answer your wish to walk. But He may have other answers for you. Look—Anh and you can't walk; I can walk. But you have better brains than I have. You and Anh are going to be able to do things with your brains that I can't do with mine."

Tich grinned at her. "Listen, Ma, next time you talk to God, you tell Him it's okay to take brains back and give me legs." They laughed.

"What so funny in there?" Anh called as he came clumping across the hall on his crutches. Entering the kitchen he stubbed both toes. He teetered, wobbled, got rid of the crutches, and landed on the palms of his hands. Then he placed the crutches upright and laboriously climbed them to the standing position.

"That was a pretty fancy dance step you did as you went down," Dorothy said. "Where'd you learn it?"

"Make it up myself," Anh grinned. "Maybe show you new one tomorrow. What laughing about?"

"Tich wants God to take his brains and give him back his legs."

"God make deal like that?"

"I don't think so."

Anh's face sobered. "Maybe God already give us deal. We in this family, ain't we?"

Dorothy kissed his cheek. "If that was a deal, I got the best part of it," she said.

Five years later, she knew better than ever that this was true.

four

Dᴏʀᴏᴛʜʏ ʜᴀᴅ ꜰɪɴɪsʜᴇᴅ scouring and storing the few pans from breakfast on that July 1975 morning, and was now putting together a casserole of leftovers. She liked it when she could prepare the evening meal in the morning so her time would be freer later. She also liked making meals from leftovers, and often planned the quantities for the first meal to allow for a reprise. It was leg of lamb this time, the final portion of the last lamb delivery from the butcher who kept her freezers supplied with meat bought in quarters or halves or wholes. He was a longtime friend and gave her a friendly price. She cut up what was left on the big bone—not as much as she'd hoped—and added sliced carrots, tomatoes, celery, green peppers, stock, herbs, and seasoning. Looking it over, she added more stock and water and threw in some raw rice. It would all cook together later.

Cooking was never a chore to her, and she could cook as easily for eighteen as eight; it made no difference. If she was too busy at the end of a day to do it, Bob took over the job, or Melanie, and sometimes Tich and Anh took a turn by preparing a Vietnamese dinner.

Dorothy didn't mind other chores, like laundry, which was easy enough to fit in among other tasks; and the younger kids regularly helped with the sorting and folding at the end. But cleaning house almost defeated her, with eleven rooms and six baths. When she could, she hired help for this, but the turnover was high with such a house and such a household, and from time to time Dorothy did without. Then everyone pitched in and somehow the house survived.

She could hear the kids playing in the family room. The room had been built as a formal dining room originally, but it had never been used that way by this family. The walls from floor to ceiling were covered with paintings done by the children through the years: charcoal sketches, oils, acrylics. Sometimes a Ping-Pong table was set up, but at the moment the space was occupied by an old dining table, used for games and for folding laundry, and four smaller plastic tables. There was an upright piano and an ancient trunk for storing toys.

Bob had contributed a new coloring book recently. Tuning in on the ongoing conversation, Dorothy heard, "Koreans like to color a lot, and I'm a Korean." That was Wendy.

And Karen: "I know. In coloring it doesn't matter what you are. I'm American and I like to color."

Dorothy called from the kitchen, "J.R., I haven't heard you at the piano yet. You'd better do your hand exercises. Please don't make me remind you." J.R. had developed "crutch hand" from using his crutches incorrectly. He had sagged against them, letting his entire weight be supported by the top crosspieces under his armpits. The pressure had affected two nerves that ran to his hand, and he had lost some muscular power.

A car pulled into the driveway: Tich and Anh returning from delivering newspapers. They always saved one copy of the *Tribune* to bring home. The car stopped abruptly at the top of the steep incline that led down to the outdoor play area and vegetable garden. Dorothy heard a thud against the side door of the house, then the car went on down the drive. Tich and Anh were going to work in the garden. It was one of their regular jobs to help Bob with the vegetable growing; they had come from small farming villages in Vietnam, so they were used to the work and they liked it. Bob had reminded them last night that the new lettuce needed thinning.

Dorothy didn't see why they were in such a rush to begin that they couldn't bring the paper into the house instead of tossing it at the side door, and she started to call out, "Please bring the newspaper in, boys," when she realized they were gone.

Then she smiled to herself. Talk about déjà vu. . . . "Bring the newspaper"—those words, and the sound of the paper thudding from the toss, were an echo from years back, in the late fifties, when Marty was a little boy. A child's terror, trembling, sweating, and screaming were new to her then—and just as new were the extremes of excitement and joy she felt when that child at last overcame his fears and discovered his own courage.

Choong Soong Park, whom Ted and Dorothy Atwood renamed Martin, had been carried screaming in the hours before dawn from a plane at San Francisco International Airport in February 1957, by a woman from the orphanage at Seoul, where he had been since a policeman had found him on a heap of garbage early in 1955. It had taken two and a half years—about the age of Marty himself—after Dorothy and Ted had first decided to adopt a child to get one. After those months upon months of frustrations and false hopes and delays, when finally Marty was put into her arms, Dorothy burst into tears of joy and relief.

The children were delighted with this small creature in the pointed slippers and crocheted cap. To them he seemed like a doll or a toy. He was tiny, all head and stomach, with spindly arms, and legs so thin and weak he couldn't stand. They found that his appetite was ravenous and noticed, too, that as he finished the food he was given, he squirreled away the last mouthfuls inside his cheeks, as if to insure against future hunger. He got over this habit quickly. But there was another problem that took him much longer to overcome.

From the moment he had been handed into her arms, Marty had an obsessive attachment to Dorothy. At first he wanted to be held all the time, and whenever she put him down he burst into tears and screams. She cooked to his screams, made beds to his screams. When finally he was able to endure bodily separation from her, he still could not bear to have her out of his sight. She was a virtual prisoner, and no matter what she or Ted or the children did in their efforts to deal with Marty's fears, the tantrums went on.

One day about three months after Marty's arrival, Dorothy was sitting out on the back patio while he played in the sandbox nearby. When she heard the afternoon newspaper land on the porch at the front of the house, she had an idea. She asked Marty to get it for her.

He set out willingly over the graveled driveway, looking back at her with every step. But the moment he rounded the corner of the house and was out of her sight, he ran back with a shriek to her arms, trembling and sweating.

The next week Dorothy again asked Marty to fetch her the paper. The result was the same. She unhurriedly tried various ploys:

"Marty, let's walk to the porch together and get the paper and bring it back."

"This time you sit here in my chair and I'll go get the paper. Just wait here for me and I'll be back in a minute."

"Marty, I'll walk you halfway round the house. Then I'll go back and wait for you to bring me the paper."

After continual failure that left Marty trembling and whimpering she stopped for a week, then again said, "Marty, please bring me the paper." He started out again. Dorothy sat and listened. She could gauge his progress by the sound of his shoes scraping the gravel of the driveway. One time it was four steps—then that scream of terror and back he ran, shaking and crying. The next time it was six steps. Then he regressed to three or four steps, and sometimes he couldn't even turn the corner out of her sight. On the days when he'd made progress, Dorothy announced it at the dinner table and the family praised and encouraged him.

Finally, one hot June afternoon in 1958, after thirteen months of repeated failure, it happened. Dorothy was sitting reading a magazine on the patio and Marty announced, as he always did, "I'm going to do it today."

"That's fine, honey," she answered without looking up. She heard the usual sound of his footsteps on the gravel. She was suddenly aware of how many there were. She froze. Was he going to make it? The crunch of shoes on gravel stopped. Was he about to turn back or had he reached the lawn between the driveway and the front porch? *Please, God* . . .

Then she heard: "Mommy, I got the paper!"

She ran to meet him, picked him up, danced around and around with him. He was covered with sweat and crying, this time in triumph, not terror, and her tears mingled with his. Still holding him, she went inside and called Ted at his office, and he came straight home.

The whole family celebrated that night. The children festooned the house with congratulatory signs, and Dorothy made Marty's favorite chicken for dinner and baked a big cake.

During dinner Mimi asked, "Marty, how did you ever do it?"

"I gather up all my braveness," Marty answered, grinning and glowing.

For the next several days Dorothy anxiously waited for Marty to relapse. He didn't. A week later she knew his braveness was firmly gathered and the victory complete when she heard herself calling out the kitchen window, "Marty! Don't touch that gate! I told you to stay in our yard. If you can't, you'll have to play in the house."

Would it have taken so long, Dorothy wondered now, seventeen years later, as she stared out the kitchen window, if she'd been a little tougher with Marty? Could that long torture both he and she endured have been cut short? Sunee's fears had been much more quickly conquered. . . . There was no answer, she decided; every child was different, and what you learned about one didn't necessarily apply to the next. Kim, for example, the second child she and Ted had adopted, had always been hard to fathom—the only one of the kids who remained guarded, basically uncommunicative, so that she was never certain what he was thinking or feeling. She didn't suppose she ever would really know him now. He had been gone for four and a half years—and in another sense for much longer than that—and now he was twenty-two and had recently told Dorothy that he was about to get married.

Kim's adjustment to his new life had required no such marathon of patience as Marty's. His coming, too, was preceded by the inevitable months of "home study" (and approval), plus delays and frustrations. Dorothy had finally telephoned directly to the director of the Child Placement Service in Seoul, explaining that she and Ted had originally requested two boys, four years ago, and they were still waiting for the second one. "I am an impatient and stubborn woman," she'd said. "If we don't hear from you soon, my husband and I will come to Korea and sit on your doorstep and probably freeze to death in your winter and you will be responsible for our deaths." Her tone had been light, but it produced results.

Within a few weeks she received a photograph of Kim Sung Kil, six, and the information that he was "born of a Korean mother and G.I. He has good looking feature with much of a husky look. Very intelligent and physically well developed. No specific bad manner is developed." His mother had tried to keep him as long as possible. When she finally accepted the fact that his mixed parentage would prejudice his future in Korea, she handed him over to the orphanage. He had been there only three weeks when Dorothy had made her telephone call to Seoul.

Kim was handsome and bright—if obviously stunned by all that had happened to him—and, after the first couple of weeks of a wooden passivity that was alarming, he developed well. Nothing seemed to upset him much, and when Ted died and Dorothy moved the family to Piedmont, Kim quickly outshone his brother Marty at school. Teachers and outsiders spoke of Kim's "intelligence," while Marty they dismissed as "cute." Despite their common Korean origin, he and Marty had discovered no mutual bond, and in fact Kim usually looked down on the younger boy.

When Kim was sixteen, through an acquaintance of Dorothy's he came to the attention of film director Robert Altman and was given a role in the movie M*A*S*H. He spent eight glorious weeks on the set in movieland—which, Dorothy later decided, was the beginning of the end. There he went from her carefully ordered household where he was expected to conform to the rules and assume tiresome chores—like making his bed, earning his spending money, respecting curfews, and the rest—to a life where, it seemed, his every whim was indulged. By the time the making of M*A*S*H was over, Kim was complaining that he didn't have a car of his own, that all his friends had more than he did, that other mothers didn't tell their kids what to do and when they could come and go. And by the time Bob arrived on the scene Dorothy's relationship with him had badly deteriorated.

Bob—who liked to say to Dorothy, "One of the reasons I married you was the free bonus: nine kids"— had no illusions about instant fatherhood. He knew that it would be a while before he was established as anything beyond, first, "the man Mom is dating," and then, after their marriage in June 1970, her tolerated consort.

The children responded to him variously: Melanie, at ten the youngest, and the readiest to welcome him, soon found he did not conform to her image of a father—a composite of her brothers' and sisters' fond memories of Ted plus the unreal father of TV situation dramas who was there only to play games, fix bikes, and yield to a daughter's every whim. Tich and Anh had always been polite and nice to him, and they remained precisely that, as if they were guests in what was now his house as well as Dorothy's. (He did not then know the anxieties they were feeling about their future in the new setup.) Bob hoped eventually to be able to be helpful to Marty, who at sixteen was always bumbling and uncertain, tripping over furniture and school authority alike, an indifferent student, frequently in trouble, and continuously a victim of Kim's jibes. Marty liked him, Bob felt, but there was no close communication.

It seemed at first that Bob would succeed in penetrating Kim's habitual reserve; they conversed animatedly as they did chores together: painting a room, putting up bookshelves, sealing leaks in the sun porch roof. But Bob soon found Kim expected him to be an ally against some of Dorothy's long established house rules—and this was a role Bob firmly rejected. He also joined Dorothy in trying to get Kim to go easier on Marty.

"Kim, why do you keep telling Marty he's stupid? Why do you keep making him feel lousy?"

"I guess I'm too rough on him. He's really a great guy."

"Then why do you do it?"

"He knows I'm kidding."

"Put yourself in his shoes."

"It wouldn't bother me. I know I'm not stupid."

With Kim's attacks at home and a pattern of past failure at the Piedmont school where, it seemed, Marty had just been marking time, Bob and Dorothy decided Marty should be given a fresh chance in another environment. They enrolled him in a Quaker school in Northern California but this didn't work out either. Shortly after he got there he was picked up by the police on a marijuana charge. Bob and Dorothy drove up to appear with him in court and he was placed on probation. They were upset but not angry. They knew Marty wasn't a "bad" boy; if a hundred boys were carrying marijuana and the police picked out one to search, sure enough it would be Marty. After another month or so, Marty dropped out of school and returned home. The following spring, in 1971, he went to live in Hawaii with Dorothy's eldest son Mike, who had a job with Royal Hawaiian Airlines and worked in a restaurant as well. Mike promised that he would do whatever he could to help "get the kid's head on straight."

Dorothy was grateful. After the fall and winter she'd gone through, it was nice to know that at least somebody's head was going to be straightened out. Marty had, as it turned out, been the least of her problems. It was Kim who brought her trouble that she had never imagined possible.

There had never been any question about it: every child in the family had always shared in the work of keeping the household going, and every child, from the early teens on, had spare-time and summer jobs to help support themselves while they were at school and later through college. Bob and Dorothy were not hard up; he had a good job with an Oakland engineering firm, she had some income from what Ted had left her, and her lecture fees helped with their expenses. But Bob, as well as Dorothy, wanted all the children to learn that money did not come free; it had to be earned.

When Bob said that summer, "Kim, get off your tail and go out and look for a job," the answer he got was, "I don't see why I have to. I've got a father now, and fathers find jobs for their sons." Taken aback, Bob corrected that assumption quickly, but Kim did nothing on his own about a job.

Then he announced that he didn't want to return in the fall to the college preparatory school in Carmel where Dorothy had sent him the year before with money made from M*A*S*H. He wanted to go back to Piedmont High.

Dorothy and Bob wouldn't hear of it. The prep school was highly rated, and a good record there would enable Kim to enter a top college. Later they realized they'd made a mistake, but by then it was too late.

Kim left home only a few days after their argument. The note in his room read: "I've gone. I don't know where I'm going yet and don't know when I'll be back. There's no use calling the police."

They decided not to call the police but to try to locate him themselves. Five weeks later they learned he was staying at the summer cottage of a friend at Lake Tahoe, nearly 200 miles away. Dorothy asked that he be sent home, but he didn't appear. Finally she and Bob went to the police—to a sergeant who knew her family and promised not to pick Kim up but only to let them know if he discovered his whereabouts.

A week later the sergeant told them Kim had been seen in Piedmont and was staying at the home of a close friend. And when school opened, Kim was seen standing in line to register. Bob called the principal's office, rushed to the school, and brought Kim home.

"What's happened to you?" Dorothy blurted. "How could you do this? Why haven't you had the decency to get in touch with us? And what were you doing standing in that line at school?"

"I'm going to Piedmont High."

"You are not."

Bob said, "You're a minor and we are responsible for you. And you have responsibilities. You have responsibilities to the feelings of your mother. Have you no concern for her? Don't you think you owe her the respect of telling her why you want to leave, where you want to go, and what you intend to do?"

"No."

Dorothy said, "Forget me. You owe me nothing. But you do owe something to the memory of your father who loved you and taught you what family love is and believed in you and wanted so much for you."

Kim replied he owed nothing to Ted's memory. "I don't owe anything to anybody. Everything I am I made myself."

Bob grabbed Kim by the shoulders. "You made you what you are? Are you proud of it?"

"Yes, I'm very proud of myself."

"What are you proud of?"

"I'm free to think as I feel, do as I feel, and not conform to anybody else's standards."

Dorothy was crying. Bob said, "You're not going to upset your mother anymore. You're proud of yourself. Go ahead and do what you're proud of."

After Kim left, Dorothy asked Bob, "What's going to happen now?"

"We'll get him back—at least long enough to find out what he wants to do."

Bob called the home where Kim had been staying

and talked with the father. Bob told him that there had been a family argument, and he wanted Kim to return home for a talk. The father said that Kim was upset and that it wasn't a good idea for him to talk just then. Dorothy then got on the phone and said she wanted to straighten out some difficulties with her son. The response was that Kim and he agreed that the time was not proper for the boy's return.

Dorothy hung up, confused and angry. "What's going on? A stranger is telling me I can't see my own son. What do I do? Kidnap him? I'm having the worst problem in my life with one of my children and some pompous bastard is telling me I can't have the chance to deal with it. My God!"

Bob said soothingly, "I'll call again tomorrow. We'll work it out."

During the following week Bob talked with the father several times and was told that Kim felt he had been badly mistreated and wanted now to live with the other family. Again he and Dorothy were refused when they asked to see Kim, and Dorothy herself phoned the father threatening to call the police. The father replied that Kim could not be forced to return if he didn't wish to.

Dorothy could not believe what was happening. She knew from Kim's earlier descriptions that this friend's household was far more casual and indulgent than her own. Although she had disagreed with their ways of doing things, she had not said so to Kim, for she felt a family's life-style was its own business. It was painfully obvious to her now that Kim preferred that other environment.

This fact was confirmed when Bob arranged for Kim to discuss the problem with the family's minister.

Kim wanted to stay where he was. He didn't want to return to rules, chores, and discipline. He was tired of being treated like a child. Living with the family had become unbearable to him, he said.

Next they persuaded Kim, through the minister, to spend a few weeks away in a different home, at a friend's house in Oregon where Kim had a standing invitation. They hoped the experience might give him a different perspective on the whole situation. It seemed to, for when Dorothy, with trembling hands, dialed the Oregon number some time later and told Kim she loved him and hoped he'd come home, he agreed.

On his return Dorothy referred only once to the past: "I'm sorry we pushed so hard about the school. I didn't realize how important it was for you to go to Piedmont High. A family sure has ups and downs and hurts, but it's great when we all come back together again."

"It sure is," Kim agreed.

But not for long. The same pattern of rebellion and resistance resumed, and finally, just after the turn of the year, Kim left, with the parting message "I love you, but I feel this is the best move for all concerned." By now Dorothy could not disagree, and she wrote back sending her understanding, approval, and love.

A few weeks later she received a letter from Kim's new family asking her to provide money for his room and board. Teenagers cost money, Dorothy was told, and the letter went on to say that a boy Kim's age should really be allowed to have a car of his own. Dorothy was infuriated. "Let Kim go out and earn his own car like his brothers and sisters have done!" she exclaimed to Bob. Her answer to the letter was a flat refusal to send money; she also pointed out that Kim could contribute to costs on his own, through the money he made giving guitar lessons.

In February the father of Kim's new family informed Bob that he was going to submit a petition to the courts to be appointed Kim's legal guardian in accordance with Kim's wishes. Kim was eligible for the draft. He planned to take out a loan for his college tuition. He felt that he had to have a guardian with whom he could discuss problems. He had no desire to talk with Dorothy or Bob, and written communication didn't seem practical to him.

There was no easy way for Bob to break this latest development to his wife. Dorothy couldn't comprehend it. "It can't be," she pleaded with Bob. "I've never heard of such a thing. I'm his mother. Can a kid tell his parents, 'I don't like you anymore. From now on So-and-So is going to be legally in charge of me'?"

"No, of course not," Bob said, but he didn't really know.

Their attorney told them that under California law a child could petition for a change of legal guardianship. If they chose to oppose the petition, the case would go to trial. In the attorney's opinion a court battle would end in victory for the DeBolts.

Night after night Dorothy and Bob talked about the change in legal guardianship. To fight it would mean involving the whole family—the other children would be called upon to testify, and it would be painful and ugly. There was already too much pain. Dorothy and Bob's nerves were raw from worry, hurt, and endless discussions. Once, when Dorothy asked Bob if he had really explored every possible solution, he punched a door in anger and turned white with pain. Hospital X-rays showed he'd fractured his hand.

Finally they decided not to go to trial. It wouldn't bring back Kim, and it was pointless to fight out of pain and anger. Instead, they went to their attorney's office to work out the financial details of the transfer of legal guardianship.

"Kim mentioned several bank accounts," the lawyer said.

"Yes," Dorothy said. "Three. Nearly fourteen hundred dollars."

The lawyer's expression told her he was under the impression that considerably more than that was involved. "He believes that a share of certain properties are due him."

"No, Ted's will left the properties to me."

"He says that you mentioned several times a legacy left to him by his deceased father. He wants it turned over to him now."

Dorothy stared blankly. Then sudden understanding hit her. She had often in the past spoken of the children's inheritance, meaning simply the feelings of love, compassion and concern for other human beings which Ted had instilled in them. Through all these years, Kim had taken the literal meaning of the word.

She quickly arose, saying, "I'm going to be sick." With her hands to her mouth she ran out of the office to the corridor washroom. The remainder of the conversation with the attorney didn't register on her. She felt utterly crushed and humiliated.

The grim paperwork still remained to be done, and there was another visit to the attorney's office when Dorothy heard incredulously the financial demands made on Kim's behalf by the new family. She was beyond struggling. She agreed to pay for Kim's hospitalization insurance and medical expenses, and to transmit to the new family Kim's monthly share of her widow's Social Security benefits and Ted's veteran's pension, plus $75 a month of her own money, for Kim's support. Kim's bank accounts were also transferred to his new guardian.

For a long time Dorothy thought her wounds would never heal. She would always bear the scars, though she and Kim had been reconciled at last at Thanksgiving 1974. During the time between, when she could think about it again, she had been struck by the irony that the insignificant sum for which the legal action had been taken came almost entirely from Ted— Kim's father to whose memory Kim had said he owed nothing.

Sunee had come a few months later. "Thank you, God, for Sunee," Dorothy said aloud in the kitchen. And even now it warmed her to think of the letter her oldest daughter Mimi had written in connection with Sunee's prospective adoption. Mimi had been working in Europe that summer, and on her return she found the social worker's request for her approval of a new addition to the family—the formality necessary to protect the other children's interests in any future inheritance.

The social worker, unasked, had sent Dorothy a copy of Mimi's reply. It read:

> My parents have spoken many times of their desire to adopt another young child. Before the death of my father, Ted Atwood, both he and my mother voiced a desire to take in a child whose health was impaired in some form or another. When my mother and my present father, Mr. DeBolt, were first informed of the possibility of adopting a young Korean-American handicapped girl, I was one of the first to know. I was as

thrilled and delighted as they. I too felt fortunate that we had been given the opportunity to, in our small way, reach out a hand in love to mankind.

Sharing is one of the strongest and most positive ideals to come out of my upbringing. We always shared at home. As far as sharing any inheritance, there can be no question in my mind. I feel it an affront to me and my parents to even mention sharing legal inheritance rights. Our inheritance has taught us just that—to share. And how can you measure an inheritance of love? . . .

I am lucky to have such parents as mine. Any child who comes into their home will be fortunate to feel the warmth of their love even for a short while. I fully approve of any new young one they wish to take in. I will welcome any and all with open arms as brother and sister.

Let it be known that I give a hearty and unconditional stamp of approval to my parents in this new act of love.

five

Both Dorothy and Bob often talked to God out loud, saying "Thank you, God" whenever something good happened or "Please" when they hoped it would. Occasionally Dorothy said, "Please, God, just one crisis at a time, all right?"

As if the troubles with Marty and Kim were not enough, during the winter of 1970–1971 there was another crisis to deal with. Sunee's greatest tutors, Tich and Anh, who taught her to be free to move, had almost been forcibly removed from the DeBolt family before Sunee ever joined it.

The two boys were by then thoroughly secure with Bob. At first they'd been uncertain about Dorothy's new husband, who, they assumed, was automatically the supreme authority in the family. Would he want to keep them? Would he want to pay for their food and clothing? Often during the summer following the marriage they had talked about it alone in their room. They believed that a forced return to Vietnam would be a death sentence. They couldn't farm. They had no skill that was any use to their families in the villages. Their communities could not provide them with drugs, urological equipment, prosthesis repairs, or medical care. But they felt they couldn't ask Bob to define their status in the family. They simply had to wait for whatever would happen to them.

Bob had had no inkling of these anxieties. It was inconceivable to him that the boys would return to their homeland until the war ended and they had developed skills to make them independent. But it never occurred to him to put this view into words.

Bob had seen signs of tension in the boys, especially Tich, but he had no way of recognizing the cause. When Tich got angry with Anh, or Melanie, or Marty, the boy nurtured the grudge for weeks. Dorothy, so closely involved with the two boys, had talked with Bob about them and his own observations confirmed what she'd said.

Tich could be caustic, and he was sometimes a cruel tease. But he could also be shrewd and wise and thoughtful. Sometimes he showed traits of strength and decisiveness that made him superior to all the forces of war and disease that had attempted to destroy him. At other times he seemed helpless and utterly vulnerable, a child wanting to cry for all the hurt that had been inflicted on him. His reactions were extravagant, ranging from the extremes of deepest sadness to radiant happiness that was expressed by an astonishingly wide and engaging smile. Anh's moods, as expressed by his strong regular features, were less exaggerated and in some ways more readable. He was sensitive to affront, and he harbored deep doubts about his ability to cope with the world around him. He hid the pain that frequently gnawed at him. He also suppressed anger, afraid to take a chance on hurting anyone's feelings.

One night the two were playing chess. Anh was

beating Tich, who was the superior player and did not take losing gracefully. In his irritation Tich knocked over several chessmen. After a quick exchange of angry words Tich swung at Anh, giving him a bloody nose. Then Bob heard them rolling on the floor, braces clanking, shouting curses at each other. Bob pulled them apart. Both boys were crying in rage.

Some weeks later—Tich was still not talking to Anh—the family was having dinner on the backyard patio. Near the end of the meal Tich made a cruel comment to Melanie, and Dorothy coldly told him that he owed her an apology for it. Tich was silent. When the family returned to the house he remained outside.

After a time Bob went out to him. Tich was standing at a retaining wall with his back turned.

"Don't you think you'd better come in?" Bob said. He saw the boy's shoulders shaking. He walked to him. Tich was crying. Bob said, "Come on, Tich, our scolding wasn't that bad."

Tich began crying harder, leaned over the wall, and lost his supper. Bob put his arm around the boy's shoulder until he finished vomiting. Tich shook a crutch and sobbed, "Why this happen to me?"

Bob could feel his frustration and anger over the disability that trapped and humiliated him. "It's going to get better, Tich," he said.

"When get better?"

"Each week you're getting stronger and doing more things."

"Why Mom take me into this house?"

Bob said, "Because she cares about you. She loves you."

"Why you care how I feel?"

"Because I love you, too."

70

"Why you love me? I not born to you."

"That doesn't matter," said Bob. "It just isn't important. We were all brought together and we are together just the same as if you had been born to us."

Without being aware of it, Bob finally had answered Tich's and Anh's unspoken question about where they stood in the family.

The problem that cropped up in the spring of 1971 had to do with the agreement between the Committee of Responsibility and the South Vietnamese government; it stipulated that the boys would remain in the United States for treatment and then return to their homeland. The United States had granted them a six months' visitor's visa, and this had already been extended several times.

Dorothy got a telephone call from an officer of COR's Bay Area chapter telling her that it was now time for the boys to go back. If they remained much longer they would surely lose their "Vietnameseness" and with it their interest in returning.

"I don't think they're ready to go back yet," Dorothy said. "Anh's family was wiped out by the war. Your own people told us that. Tich has a mother, but he needs more medical care. He still gets pressure sores. He still doesn't have the right brace design for him. And he still gets occasional urinary infections."

"We've arranged for the children to get medical care in Saigon."

"That's no help," said Dorothy. "Tich's family lives in a rural village."

"We're prepared to help," the woman said. "We have a place in Saigon called Vietnam House where the returning children live while learning a craft or a trade."

"We'll discuss it with the boys," Dorothy said.

"Yes, explain to them that it's time for their trip home. They knew their stay here was temporary."

"I think the decision depends on a lot of factors."

When Dorothy and Bob told the boys about the call, they were silent. Bob suggested that Tich and Anh talk it over between themselves. That evening they told Dorothy and Bob that they didn't feel ready to return. They wanted further education, which would be impossible for them to obtain in South Vietnam. They had no skills yet that would enable them to make money in that war-torn country.

Bob said, "That's fine with us. Your decision is probably going to cause a hassle with the Committee, but we'll fight it out. If you don't want to go back at this time, as far as we're concerned, you are not going to be forced to go back."

"No, no," Tich said. "If we cause trouble, we go back. You do so much for us already. We no want to cause you trouble. We go back."

"The only trouble you cause us is when you talk like that," Bob said. "Just tell us this: do you guys want to go back to Vietnam eventually?"

Anh said, "Yes. Want to go back to help. Not want to go back to be a burden. Like to go back as engineer. Do something to help my country!"

"I feel same," Tich agreed. "Thinking of becoming a doctor."

Bob nodded. "Okay. That's it." After the boys left, he considered the conversation. If they returned to South Vietnam now, what could they do? They would indeed be a burden. If they completed their education, they could return, earn a living, and possibly make a contribution to their countrymen. Anh an engineer?

Maybe. Or suppose he became a brace maker—what a need he could fulfill! And Tich a physician? Even if he didn't get into medical school, he could still be trained to be an expert laboratory technician or physical therapist. Bob decided that under no circumstances would the boys be returned against their will.

He knew it would not be easy to deny the demand of the Committee, which was, after all, the legal guardian of the boys and held their passports and visas. The DeBolts were only temporary guardians. If the visas were not renewed, the Immigration and Naturalization Service would order Tich's and Anh's deportation.

Bob decided that he had to get possession of the passports—and the only way right now was by a ruse. Dorothy telephoned the executive secretary of the Committee and told her that the family was planning a vacation in Mexico at the beginning of the upcoming school summer vacation. The vacation was no problem as far as Tich and Anh were concerned, the woman said; she had to be away from the office for several weeks and no action would be taken on the boys until her return.

After her departure Bob visited the Committee's office and told a woman who was there to answer the phone that the vacation plans were set and he needed the boys' passports to obtain Mexican tourist cards for them. She cheerfully turned them over to him. He drove directly to his bank and put the passports in his safety deposit box.

He and Dorothy immediately called the South Vietnamese consul general in San Francisco, Dr. Luong Nhi Ky, and asked for an appointment. Dr. Ky, a small, delicate man, listened earnestly as Bob and Dorothy described the plight of Tich and Anh. He next met the boys. After a lengthy private conversation with Tich and Anh in his office, he told Dorothy and Bob that he unequivocally agreed with their attitude. "You are not their original parents," he said, "but you are the parents who have given them hope and opportunity. I will recommend to my government that the boys continue to live with you and that you be given full responsibility for them. You will have to deal with the people at the Immigration and Naturalization Service about visas. I can't help you there."

After checking regulations Bob concluded that Tich and Anh should apply for student visas, which would have to be renewed annually. He filled out various forms, listing Dorothy and himself as the boys' guardians, and appended financial statements, a guarantee to support the boys and pay for their education, and a statement from the local school of their status as full-time students. Bob made several trips to the Immigration and Naturalization Service office in San Francisco, where he endured the bureaucratic runarounds. It took months of Bob's persistent pleas before the student visas were granted.

Meanwhile the DeBolts and COR continued to discuss and argue the boys' fate. Nothing was resolved. COR insisted that the boys had to return. The DeBolts refused to release the boys from their care. On July 24, 1971, the executive secretary wrote them a letter intended to settle the issue:

> Since my talk with Bob the other day I have thought much about the return of Anh and Tich—in fact, I have thought of little else. I have reviewed the cases of other children returned, their experiences and those of foster parents, trying to put my own feelings aside and considering, so far as this is humanly possible, what is best for the child. All our experience, our best

information is that the children should be returned; that their readjustment to Vietnamese life, their ability to handle their situations there, are better when they can be returned in the shortest possible time.

It is your feeling that their chances will be vastly greater if they remain in this country until they finish high school, gain skills and return in four years. In four years these children will be young men, they will be American in their thinking, their orientation and in their consciousness. If they now find such richness in their life with you, in the beautiful American family at its finest and most unique which you provide, they are not going to be more eager to leave it in four more years. Compelling reasons will be there to delay the return further, or they will make application for citizenship and the Americanization will be complete.

There is not a family who has not at some point wanted to keep the children longer—for the best interests of the child; and there is not a child who has not at some time or other asked to remain here. Other parents, though they knew, too, the conditions under which they took on this terrible responsibility, have wanted to adopt children. But we are not in the business of exporting children.

These children are the last natural resource of Vietnam. You, me, all of us have worked to save them and we do not intend to let them die. What you have done for these particular boys, and for the Committee of Responsibility—which is other people like yourselves—is of a value one cannot possibly estimate. Dorothy has a heart like an apartment house and Bob, apparently, has just added a few more units, and I can only see for you further expansion. You have given the boys, Tich and Anh, strength and enrichment as they have learned to live without legs. The future none of us can insure, we can only help them to accept it, to cope with it. It is a part of Vietnamese life to live without crises; events flow into each other, departures, reunions, birth and death. It is only Westerners who have brought the trauma, the cutting of the sequence. In Vietnam House, Vietnam, the children face life alone, but supported by each other. What has proved most remarkable is the normalcy of their return. It is for this now that we must work together.

Dorothy replied:

We deeply regret the position you've taken in regard to Tich and Anh's future. Tich and Anh, through no fault of their own, have already been paralyzed in body. We adamantly refuse to submit them to that paralysis of spirit which would inevitably follow their forced return to Vietnam at this time. We care not one whit whether Tich and Anh are Vietnamese or American. We do care that they are human beings!

I do not wish to fight. On the other hand, neither will I flee from battle. Bob and I will not cease until we have exhausted every possible means of assisting Tich and Anh toward the future they seek.

You have no right, nor indeed do *we*, to determine the potential scope of these boys' lives. That choice is *theirs*. God knows we owe them that!

Dorothy didn't want to break with the Committee. She supported it and believed in the immeasurable value of its work in salvaging terribly wounded children. For nearly two years she had made impassioned fund-raising speeches on its behalf. But she and her husband had committed themselves to giving the boys a fair chance in life. That chance went beyond medical treatment. It meant giving the boys the opportunity to develop useful, productive, satisfying skills that would make them independent of charity and pity.

In an effort to have her view understood, she wrote

76

to the Committee's national chairman in Washington, D.C.:

Tich and Anh came to me, then a widow with seven children, in 1969. They were typical of the Vietnamese paraplegic children with whom COR has dealt. Their bodies were painfully thin, their moods uncertain and bewildered, and urological, orthopedic and dermatological problems were prevalent. Within two months of their arrival here Tich and Anh were attending our public junior high school.

They began on a limited basis, half-day with all courses on one floor. Within one year each had achieved full attendance with no special dispensation for their physical or scholastic handicaps. They carry the same number of units as all normally capable students, climb the same stairs, and cover all levels of the hilly terrain upon which Piedmont Junior High School is located. If the halting motion of brace and crutch slows them down, they receive tardy slips, precisely the same as other students. The F's, D's, and Incompletes of their first reports have ended. June, 1971, found them with grades of A's, B's, and C's. This has been accomplished despite fairly frequent absences for treatment of decubiti [pressure sores] involving surgical procedures, urinary infections, and the constant fittings for braces, etc. This type of medical treatment will to some degree be never ending. Despite enormous progress made, their physical conditions are tenuous. To return them to the uncertainties of a current Vietnam is to jeopardize their very lives. It is not we alone who make this judgment. This is the expert opinion of their doctors as well as orthopedic specialists with whom we work. Please do not suggest the plans for their continued medical treatment in Vietnam. I have read your statement that COR is in serious financial trouble. I have read Dr. Dickstein's appraisal of the lack of just about any kind of medicine in

Vietnam right now, his statement that "hospital facilities are abysmal," that "some poor kids just lie on cots and languish there for years." What happens when Tich requires the next plastic surgery on his back? Will he, too, languish unattended on one of those cots? Hell, no, not if *we* can prevent it!

We are determined to support Tich and Anh in their wish to remain in America. It is our fervent hope that you, as the National Director of COR, will recognize and concern yourself with the fate of these two boys. We intend to keep Tich and Anh here. We hope to do it with your blessings. It would be so much more agreeable for all concerned that way.

But the chairman replied that the Committee was bound by a legal agreement with the Vietnamese Minister of Health to return the children when their medical care was completed.

Bob telephoned the chairman and was again told the boys would have to go back.

"We can't allow that," Bob replied. "They don't want to go back, and we won't permit anyone to force them to go back. The boys have made their decision and they have our support, and you and your people just leave them the hell alone. If you want to make a fight of this you'll get a fight."

"You do get dramatic, Mr. DeBolt."

Whether it was Bob's getting "dramatic" or simply refusing to budge, the fight was finally won. On September 20 the DeBolts received a letter from the Minister of Health in Saigon which gave them the "full responsibility of these children till they will have completed their education, provided that no objections from their parents, legal custodians or family are raised." The letter asked that "this Ministry be informed at your earliest convenience of the exact length of time you wish to have these children in your big family."

The DeBolts outlined for the minister the boys' educational plans and explained the difficulties of setting a precise time for them to reach their goals. They gave assurances of "never failing to encourage them in their nationalistic pride."

Tich had been writing to his mother in Vietnam for five months, telling her of his ambitions and asking her to agree to the DeBolts' being his legal guardians for the duration of his education, but his letters apparently never reached his village of DucDuc. So Bob wrote the mayor of Da Nang, the provincial capital, describing the difficulties in communication and asking him to see that the enclosed letter from Tich to his mother was delivered. In November 1971, Tich's mother replied, assigning legal and parental authority over her son to the DeBolts for the period of his education. Her letter ended any further need for discussion between the Committee of Responsibility and the DeBolts.

Tich and Anh were the only children brought to the States by the Committee who were not returned to South Vietnam.

Bob handed Consul General Ky the letter from Tich's mother. The consul agreed that there would be no further difficulties about the boys' completing their education.

When Bob tried to thank him, the consul said that he had only done what was right for Tich and Anh. Then he paused. "There is a favor that you could do for me."

"I'll be glad to."

"I am being recalled to Saigon for reassignment. My sister-in-law, who also works in the consulate, is also being recalled. Her husband, my brother, was killed in battle. She has her five children here and is also caring for a young nephew whose father is a government official in Saigon. All six children are in school here. Three are attending college. We would like them to remain here until their schooling is finished. The three older boys are living on their own, but I would like them to have a U.S. citizen as legal guardian. About the three younger boys: Tuoc, nine, and Dat, fourteen, are the children of my sister-in-law. Trang is her nephew. He's twelve. I was hoping that your wife and you would know of families that would permit the three younger boys to live with them."

"I'll talk with my wife about this," Bob said. "You'll hear from me tomorrow."

After Bob reported the conversation to Dorothy, they sat silent for a minute. Then, Dorothy said, "I can make phone calls and ask people, but let's not kid ourselves. What stranger is going to agree to become legal guardian to the three college boys living on their own?"

"I can't think of any parents that would," Bob said ruefully.

Dorothy made some telephone calls and reported to Bob, "Maryanne Hill said she'd take the youngest boy. That's about it."

Bob, slumped in a chair, looked at his wife. His eyes carried a slightly bemused, inquiring expression.

Her eyes crinkled in a smile. "All right, all right," she said. "The two boys can take the basement bedroom that Mike and Kim used."

At the end of February 1972 the cousins Dat and

Trang moved into the DeBolt home. The two boys, aided by the advice, warnings, and general briefings from their fellow countrymen, Tich and Anh, slipped easily into the family pattern. The younger one, Trang, was a thin, tiny boy, wary, cautious, anxious to please, fearful of making a mistake. He was unable to speak English very well, and was somewhat subservient to his older cousin. But he proved to be incredibly well coordinated—the best athlete in the family. His great love was football, though Dorothy would have been happier with him in a less rough sport. He and Melanie, the closest in age, seemed to understand each other right from the beginning—even when she seemed most unpredictable to her mother—and as time went on he developed self-confidence, became much more sure of himself than most boys his age, and was able to respond to any challenge, be it on the football field or cleaning up the kitchen. Dorothy made an agreement with the football coach: Trang could go to practice three afternoons a week, but he had to relieve Melanie of the chores the other two.

Dat, with his wavy black hair, flashing dark brown eyes, and slight, wiry build, was dynamic and indefatigable. He took a heavier load of high school courses than most other students. He scored good grades. He held three after-school jobs—paper route, yard cleanup, and service station attendant. He was an absent-minded boy, forgetting lunch half the time, leaving his books at school, but he was one of the hardest and best workers Dorothy and Bob had ever seen: efficient, enthusiastic, fast, better than most grown men. And so it seemed that each had talents to offset the other, but both had one thing in common—they were beautiful to have in the family.

Tich and Anh were devoted to exercises and weight lifting to strengthen their bodies. Both firmly believed, too, that muscles made them more attractive to the girls. Dat quickly adopted their views, and the three boys spent two hours each day exercising and pushing barbells on the basement floor. Anh and Dat also spent hours poring over body-building magazines. All four boys enjoyed each other's company and spent so much time jabbering away in Vietnamese that Dorothy had to remind Dat and Trang that they were in this country to learn English.

On the issues of Vietnamese politics, however, the two pairs were ferocious antagonists. With the Presidential election in the air, Tich and Anh were all for McGovern, for they were violently opposed to this country's participation in the war. Dat and Trang, who, unlike the other two, came from well-to-do Saigon families, were pro-Nixon. Dat especially favored the United States role and in fact wanted the country to throw more arms and men into the war.

At times the arguments between the boys grew loud and bitter and, on one occasion, Bob had to separate them before someone threw a fist. Tich was shaking with anger.

"Dat don't know what he talk about," he advised Bob. "Anh and me know war. He don't."

Bob finally reminded Tich, "I think you've forgotten that Dat's father was killed in that war. He might have just as many feelings as you have about it. It doesn't mean he's right or you're right. It just means that you should respect his feelings."

As Bob left the room he heard Tich say, "Dat, I forget that. I sorry. You lose. We lose. Everybody lose."

When Bob told Dorothy of Tich's final words, she thought, "Mike should be here." Her oldest son too had strong feelings about the war. He had risked everything for them. In September 1970, he had filed with the local draft board as a conscientious objector. He felt he was incapable of killing or contributing to killing, and that to serve even as a noncombatant would be to help the process of destruction and murder. But he would not run away. He stood up for what he believed in, and he asked that he be allowed to perform some humanitarian service. He would be willing to fly into dangerous territories to deliver food or to help build; he would not learn to destroy.

The Berkeley draft board had rejected his petition, and it had been a long struggle. Finally, on appeal, a federal court had accepted his objections to military service and he was ordered to return to Hawaii to serve as a volunteer in a school for the handicapped. He was to serve for one year on a forty-hour-a-week basis and for a second year on a half-time basis. Dorothy was immensely proud of Mike.

It was just three months, Dorothy reflected, since Mike's two years were at last creditably completed in April 1975, and she still thought with pride of the courage he'd shown in fighting for his convictions. But then, none of her kids had a corner on courage. Sunee, Karen, Wendy . . . J.R. was coming along too; all he needed was to find that extra spark in himself; and it would happen any day now. Twe and Lee? They'd only just arrived really. This afternoon could be Twe's first test in a way: Dorothy was to take her to her third in a series of eye examinations, and this one would answer the question of whether or not there was any possibility of her regaining her vision. If the answer was no, how would Twe take it?

Finished with her postbreakfast chores in the kitchen, Dorothy was back at her desk in the bedroom. By swiveling her chair she could look out the window behind her, down into the play area where the children were having a ball game under the warm July sun. J.R. was supposed to be doing his piano exercises downstairs, but now she could hardly hear him. It wasn't just the shouts of the others at play; he wasn't working. She knew beyond any doubt that he was again slumped in his wheelchair in front of the piano, his hands all but idle, his mind lost in daydreaming.

Dorothy got up and went quickly down the stairs. "J.R., daydreaming will get you nothing," she said as she walked into the family room. "But you might as well stop the piano for now. Let's go out back now. It's too nice to stay indoors all morning."

She pushed his wheelchair out the side door, dropping one by one over the three steps there, and wheeled him carefully down the steep driveway which was slightly ridged at intervals to brake the descent. Tich and Anh were nowhere in sight; they must have finished in the garden quickly.

"Hey, J.R.'s going to get into the game," ten-year-old Phong called to the others. J.R.'s sightless brown eyes lighted up. "This is home plate," Phong went on. "First base is the corner of the swings. Second base over there. Third is the corner of the box with the stringbeans growing. Come on, J.R., you can be at bat. Wendy, will you push J.R. to first base if he gets a hit?"

"All right. Just once."

Karen stationed herself at first. "Get it to me fast," she shouted at Sunee, who was covering third.

"Go on, J.R.," Dorothy said, stepping back from his chair. He wheeled himself in position at bat, his chair almost facing first.

"Ready?" Phong called.

"Ready," J. R. answered, tightening his grip on the bat.

"O.K." Phong, in an underhand pitch, softly lobbed the 10-inch ball toward the bat and yelled "Swing!" J.R. winced as the ball traveled toward him; he swung out and missed—the pitch was high.

Phong retrieved the ball and pitched again. This time J.R. connected. He gave a shout of triumph. Wendy leaped up and ran to the chair, struggling to push J.R. toward first. Phong yelled, "Roll your wheels, J.R.! Push those wheels!" Karen was hopping up and down on her plastic legs between her crutches, imploring, "Throw it, Sunee, throw it!"

As fast as she could go Sunee swung her crutches to the ball. Balancing on her braced feet for a second, she grasped it between the two rubber tips of her crutches, flipped it in Karen's direction, then quickly dropped the tips to the grass before she toppled over. The toss wasn't far enough. Phong had joined Wendy in pushing J.R. Sunee charged toward the ball and banged it with the tip of her crutch toward first base. Too late—J.R. was safe.

Nobody was ever put out, and Phong arbitrarily decided turns at bat. "O.K., now Karen bat," he said as Dorothy started back up to the house. "Hey, Mom, you want to play?" he called.

"Not right now, thanks," she said. "Maybe next time."

The kids' yells as she got to the door told her Karen had got a hit. Karen almost never missed.

six

WHEN THEY had just won their fight to keep Tich and Anh in this country and were still preparing to take Dat and Trang into the family, Dorothy and Bob were getting involved in the adoption of another child.

On a Sunday morning in early January 1972, Bob was reading the magazine section of the paper, and his attention was caught by a full-page spread of pictures of black children available for adoption. The most urgent need appeared to be that of seven-year-old Jimmy, severely crippled by cerebral palsy.

The expression in the boy's eyes held Bob. Neither he nor Dorothy had made any definite plans to seek another handicapped child for adoption, but somehow they both knew they would.

Bob passed the page to his wife. She slowly looked at the pictures and read the captions. "You thinking of Jimmy?" she asked.

"Yes. Sunee and he could be good for each other," said Bob. "Someone closer to her own age to play with."

"All right," Dorothy said, glancing back to the

page. "It says that all these children are under the care of the Spence-Chapin Adoption Service in New York City. I'll write a letter to the agency inquiring about Jimmy."

The agency quickly replied that Jimmy had been living with foster parents who had just decided to adopt him. A few days later, however, the agency's executive director, Jane Edwards, wrote Dorothy:

> We wonder if you would consider accepting another child with a very severe physical handicap, but one who is very intelligent and apparently artistically creative.
>
> The child who waits in an institution is five-year-old Karen, a little girl who is black, who is a congenital amputee involving upper and lower extremities, who uses prostheses, crutches and a wheelchair. Karen is considered to be a very bright, appealing and lovely little girl who enjoys singing and painting, which she does quite well.
>
> Your family might be the only chance Karen will ever have to leave the institution where she has been all of her young life.

The DeBolts were not at all sure. They couldn't visualize the child from the brief description, but if they really were an "only chance" they wanted to know more about her. Dorothy telephoned Mrs. Edwards, who told her that Karen had been given to a hospital by the mother a few weeks after birth: Karen had been born without legs and forearms.

In two weeks the DeBolts received a marvelously warm, obviously loving letter about Karen from the social worker handling her case. He reported that the child's right arm ended above the elbow, her left arm shortly below it. She had been fitted with a "sitting bucket" attached to her legless lower body and with two artificial legs. She had artificial arms as well, ending in metal prongs which she herself could open and close. She could get around with either crutches or a wheelchair, could eat by herself, using a swivel spoon and a fork with adjustable stops, and she could drink from a cup. The more the letter went on, the more incredible this young child seemed: she had become so proficient with the use of her hooks that she could not only brush her own teeth, but embroider, paint, draw, and write. Her teachers found her bright and eager to learn.

Karen had spent her entire life in a hospital setting. Now the hospital in which she had found love would soon have to relinquish her: it had no facilities for older children.

The social worker admitted that when he had first gone to see Karen, he was prepared to meet a severely disabled youngster, and he had wondered whether he would be able to hide his pity. But one smile from that responsive face—a smile that lit up the room—had won him over. This was a child to be loved, to be enjoyed, not pitied.

The DeBolts read the letter several times and studied the accompanying photograph of Karen. The idea of a child without arms and legs aroused discomfort and pity, but Karen's eyes showed only candor, determination, and an eagerness to be challenged.

They showed the children Karen's photograph and described her handicaps. In an offhand way Dorothy mentioned that she lived in a hospital and needed a family and a home. She watched for responses. Tich said, "She have more problems than we have."

Sunee was incredulous. "No legs *and* no arms.

Anybody can get along without legs. But you need hands."

"She manages pretty well," Dorothy pointed out. "She can eat with her hooks and stitch with an embroidery needle."

"Gee," Sunee said in surprise. "But can she run and play? Can she go as fast as I can?"

There were many more questions—all of them as to what Karen might be able to do, how she would handle something. The children generally took it for granted that she would make it: after all, they could handle handicaps.

Dorothy and Bob talked a lot about Karen together. What were the mechanics and practicalities of caring for such a child? How much direct physical assistance would she need? They were raising their children, both the able-bodied and the handicapped, to become independent, to be able to leave the house and establish their own lives. Would Karen ever be able to function in the give and take of normal society?

The difference in race didn't bother them. But how would Karen feel when she reached adolescence, a black girl with white parents? Would that add a social handicap to her other disabilities? After a time Dorothy sighed and said, "This kind of talk is futile. There are no answers. We can find out only about now, today. Tomorrow, we have to play by ear."

Both wanted the child, yet neither could say, "We've got to take the kid in," for fear of forcing the other into agreement.

Around three o'clock one morning, Bob suddenly awoke. Dorothy was crying in her sleep. He took her in his arms and woke her.

She sobbed for a moment, then was quiet.

"What was it?" he asked.

"I was dreaming of Karen," she said, slowly, reflectively. "Karen was lying on a sidewalk. She wasn't wearing prostheses. She looked like a bundle. There were a lot of people walking and hurrying along the sidewalk. Some stepped on her. Some stepped over her. Some shoved her out of the way with a foot. No one seemed to recognize that she was a human being. Karen was screaming, 'I'm here! I'm here!' but no one heard her."

Dorothy wept. "How can we let that child stay where she is? We know she exists. We can't refuse her."

Bob held her closer. "It looks like Karen has a mother and a father, and we have a daughter."

Both were relieved. Dorothy wrote Mrs. Edwards:

> We have delved into our thinking, resources (mental, physical and spiritual) and wherewithal. We have inquired about schooling, occupational therapy, etc. We have talked with other members of the family. We have considered the future, as well as the present. The consensus is that we would be greatly privileged to have Karen in our family.
>
> I understand your need for information on our family as well as our financial situation. I will send you the complete home study done last year by the caseworker handling our last adoption.

Correspondence between the two coasts fluttered slowly for months. The home study done by the California Department of Social Welfare before Sunee was placed was updated and forwarded to the New York adoption agency.

It was not until September 1, 1972, that the Spence-Chapin senior caseworker sent the DeBolts written hope that they could come east for Karen—and that would be in early October.

Dorothy and Bob spent six hours composing a scrapbook for Karen containing about three dozen pictures of the family, all of them captioned, and the house. And each child wrote a letter to Karen. Dat, who had just turned fifteen, told her about his favorite sport, track, and hoped she would run fast too. Bob took a picture of the bed she would sleep in and the corner of the room she would share with nineteen-year-old Noël. Noël was supposed to have left for college that fall, but she had postponed it for six months to help with Karen: she was the only driver Dorothy had. The scrapbook had pictures of all of them, including Yup-Yup, the mongrel they had just adopted—or, more properly, the mongrel that had adopted them. Both Dorothy and Bob had tried to make the dog stop hanging around, but both had also felt sorry enough for the animal to feed her surreptitiously, and so Yup-Yup had joined the family—named by Dat and Trang. The boys confessed the meaning of the Vietnamese name: what they had to clean up after her.

Karen responded with a scrawled note, "I love all of you except the dog," and enclosed three photographs of herself.

Dorothy wrote: "I want you to know how happy and pleased we all were to receive those beautiful pictures of you. I really didn't know you were such a pretty little girl. You look like a princess. We are all counting the days until you are with us."

Then the senior caseworker reported a delay: the hospital staff needed more time to prepare Karen for her new life. Her prostheses needed many adjustments.

The arrival of the DeBolts in New York was set for October 25.

Bob went to his boss and told him he had to take a few days off to go to New York "to pick up our new daughter." He didn't offer any details; he didn't think anyone in his company would understand why a middle-class middle-aged couple would want to take on an armless and legless black orphan.

His boss said, "Okay. Tell you what—why don't you check out an electrical contracting firm in the Washington, D.C., area for me? It has a terrific reputation and I've been wanting to look into it. Spend a day there and get a view of how they operate. I'll pay for the roundtrip plane fare for both of you."

Dorothy was bursting to talk about Karen outside the family. At a fashionable San Francisco hairdresser's salon she sat next to an acquaintance. Dorothy told her. "We're going back east in a few days to adopt another child."

"Really?" the woman responded in genuine interest. "What kind of child this time? Korean or Vietnamese or what?"

"A little black girl."

"Well, you sure go for variety," the woman said lightly. "Does she have a handicap?"

Dorothy described Karen. She saw the acquaintance didn't know how to react. The woman murmured, "Well, have a good trip," and picked up the magazine in her lap.

Dorothy also told a few other people, men and women whom she knew cared about adoptions and the need to find homes for handicapped children. She got much the same response from them: a forcedly bland expression and an uneasy comment in an attempt to conceal their shock. They didn't want to hear any more about it. They just weren't prepared for this combination of parents and child. It seemed strange, almost bizarre, to them.

On the day before their departure for the east, Dorothy was pell-melling through her chores, giving instructions to the housekeeper and the children, shopping for food, talking to Noël about meals. As she reminded Noël of the pot roast in the freezer, her mind was on the pants that had to be picked up at the dry cleaner's and the need to post on the kitchen bulletin board an itinerary giving the phone numbers at which they could be reached during each phase of the trip. The phone rang and Dorothy heard a breathless juvenile voice say, "Hi, Mom, this is Jennifer. Can I go to the playground to play with Suzie?"

"Sure, honey, but be back by five." She hung up.

"Who was that?" Noël asked her mother.

Dorothy stared at her. "My God!" she said. "I don't have a kid named Jennifer."

They landed at Dulles International Airport and took the airport bus to their hotel in Washington. Dorothy was staring straight ahead, and Bob wondered why she wasn't admiring the sight of the autumn leaves still changing color. He said, "What are you looking at?"

She bobbed her head. "That's something I'm going to have trouble with. Black hair."

"What are you talking about?"

She nodded her head toward a couple four rows of seats ahead of them: a black man and a black girl about seven or eight years old. She said, "Look at that black hair. How do you get a comb through such thick hair?"

"I don't know."

"I'll have to find out. I wonder how many times a week you wash black hair."

"I don't know. Honey, you're beginning to sound like a racist."

"Do you do it as often as white hair? Or less? It *is* different." Dorothy was in a serene, musing mood. "I'm sure Karen's prostheses match her skin," she said.

"Oh, I don't know. Have you ever seen an artificial limb that was other than white-flesh-colored?"

"No, that would look ridiculous on Karen. They'd just have to try to match her skin."

"Look. You can imagine how expensive prostheses are. Tich's last set of braces cost us more than four hundred dollars. Karen's a child, a charity case. Esthetics have got to be the last concern."

"I don't agree. They're going to care how a kid feels when she looks at herself. I bet you twenty dollars they're brown."

Bob grinned. "You're on!"

"I keep thinking about her," Dorothy continued. "What do you think her reaction'll be when we take her out of the hospital?"

Bob turned to look at the trees for a moment. "When she knows we're going to take her away from everything that's familiar to her? Fear? Insecurity?"

"Apprehension?"

"Yes. Apprehension."

During the night before the meeting with Karen, Dorothy had nightmares. She kept seeing a small black limbless body, lying helpless on the ground and people milling about oblivious to her. She saw herself at home, rushing from room to room, trying to find the child. In another dream sequence Karen's hooks kept falling off and Dorothy repeatedly pushed them back on, but the hooks could not be attached firmly to the child's arms.

Bob understood those nightmares. He too was filled with apprehension. Sunee had been an easy "yes," but Karen . . . a child barely more than a torso, and who knew how well that worked? Dorothy and he were middle-aged, taking on a six-year-old, and the age difference would never get less. They were going to be totally responsible for that human being. No matter what the agency had told them, the odds were that, since Karen had been in an institution all her life, she was so messed up emotionally that she'd spend the rest of her years—and theirs—getting straightened out. If she ever did. And they might end up just as messed up as she. But he knew deep down inside that none of these fears made a bit of difference. The answer to Karen had to be yes. There was no other answer.

In the morning two caseworkers from Spence-Chapin picked them up in front of the motel and drove them to St. Mary's Hospital for Crippled Children, supported by the Episcopal Church. They were ushered into a conference room. In a few minutes they were greeted by a file of people—nuns, the chief nurse, Karen's physician, the physical therapist, and the occupational therapist.

A nun told the DeBolts, "Karen has seen so many children come and go. She has seen them brought in by their parents and taken away by their parents. Once, when a little girl in her ward left, Karen said, 'I have a mommy and daddy, too. God just forgot where he put them.' "

"It looks like they've been found," said Bob.

Two social workers, one from Spence-Chapin and

the other from the hospital, escorted the DeBolts to a small lounge to meet Karen. The four sat and waited. Dorothy was too impatient and nervous to make conversation. She wanted to see Karen, touch her, connect with her. Bob paced, then stared out a picture window at a grassy slope still green but freckled with fallen brown leaves.

After twenty minutes, one social worker rose and said she'd find out what was detaining Karen. She returned with a young black girl on crutches and braces.

Bob greeted her. "Hi, Karen."

"I'm not Karen," the girl said, looking at him with great seriousness. "I'm Betty."

The social worker smiled and said, "Betty is Karen's best friend."

Bob felt like an idiot. The girl had legs—paralyzed—and hands. He said, "Hi, Betty," and Dorothy said, "Hello, Betty, how's Karen?"

The child returned the greeting and said, "Karen's all right."

Karen apparently had sent down her friend to scout the situation and bring back an impression of the DeBolts. The girl suddenly turned and left, trailed by the social worker.

In about ten minutes the DeBolts heard the tap of crutches outside the room and a child's voice singing. Karen appeared in the doorway with the social worker. Dorothy noticed that the prosthetic arms below the short sleeves of her bright red sweater were dark chocolate-colored. Dorothy nudged Bob. "I win our bet."

Karen took a quick look at the people in the room, buried her face in the social worker's skirt, and said, "I don't wanna go in."

The social worker slowly entered the room with

Karen timidly behind her. The DeBolts said, "Hi, Karen."

"I'm your mommy," Dorothy said softly, "and I think you're beautiful."

"And I'm your daddy," Bob said, "and you are just the way we knew you would be."

Karen flashed a brief, bright smile. The social worker showed the DeBolts several drawings Karen had made in class that day. One was a pumpkin, and Dorothy began talking about a Halloween party they would have after they got home. The social workers left, and Karen responded to questions monosyllabically in a low, husky voice.

Karen had carried into the room a toy plastic suitcase containing Barbie dolls and clothing. Bob said, "Let's play with your Barbie dolls. I think this one needs a change of dress." He sat on the floor with Karen while Dorothy watched.

Karen proudly showed off her skills with her hooks—dressing and undressing the dolls and pinning tiny earrings to their ears. She became relaxed, spontaneous. "Daddy, would you put on that doll's socks and shoes, while I put a coat and hat on this one? It's pretty chilly out today and we don't want Barbie to catch a cold."

"There," Bob said, after following instructions.

"Thank you, Daddy."

Dorothy and Bob looked at each other, and their eyes shone with tears.

They had decided to make their first visit brief, to keep the initial tension to a minimum. Dorothy said, "How about showing us your room, Karen?"

Karen packed the dolls and clothing into the toy suitcase and led the DeBolts down a corridor. She showed them how she maneuvered a ramp on her crutches and braces, how she used a crutch to flick light switches and push elevator buttons.

A nurse's aide was in her room. She turned to Karen and said, "Show your mommy and daddy how you get ready for bed."

Karen lay back on the bed. With her hooks she unbuckled the corset that held the bucket and legs to her body. She pushed herself back out of the bucket and stood the lowers at the end of the bed. Bob was momentarily shocked by the sight of Karen on one part of the bed and her legs dressed in red pants, blue socks, and red shoes standing a few feet away from her.

Karen lifted off her red sweater, unstrapped the harness of her uppers, and placed the apparatus near her legs. With her stumps she pushed off underpants in which there were no openings for legs. There she was, as she was born. Dorothy looked at Karen's nude torso, trying not to stare. It was firm and beautiful, perfectly round and smooth where legs otherwise would have extended.

Karen adeptly lowered herself off the bed and wriggled across the floor like a happy seal.

"Come on, Karen," called the aide. "Get back on the bed and show your folks how you shake that pretty little butt of yours."

Karen pulled herself up on the bed. She stood on her head, balancing herself with her stumps, and shook her hips as if she were dancing to a fast piece of rock music. Freedom from the prostheses was more than a physical release. Karen was exuberantly glad to be alive. Laughter burst out of her as the aide began to wrestle with her. Her eyes sparkled. Dorothy and Bob were astonished and moved.

After a few moments Bob said, "We'd better go now, Karen. We'll be back tomorrow afternoon to pick you up. We'll go out and have dinner. Like that?"

"Oh, yeah," Karen said, bouncing on the bed.

"She won't have her uppers tomorrow," the aide said. "They have to go to the shop for adjustments. We want everything just right when you take her home."

"That's all right," said Dorothy. "We can have dinner in the motel room."

The DeBolts spent the next morning at Spence-Chapin headquarters in Manhattan, taking care of the necessary adoption details. When they went to the hospital, they found Karen working with her physical and occupational therapists.

Her mood had changed dramatically. She was sullen. She refused to cooperate with the therapists. She would not talk with the DeBolts and hardly acknowledged their presence. Leaving the hospital wasn't going to be easy for her, they realized.

While doing exercises on a mat, Karen suddenly broke into tears. Dorothy knelt on the mat and held Karen in her arms. When Karen stopped crying, Dorothy suggested to the therapists that it might be a good idea to end the session for the day. They agreed and left.

Bob lifted Karen to his arms and said, "Hey, daughter, you feel like going for a little walk?"

Karen nodded. "But you won't take me out of the hospital, will you?"

"I don't see why not. You have your mommy and daddy with you to take care of you."

Karen asked to see her social worker. They carried the child to the social services office, where the worker cradled Karen in her arms.

Bob said, "All right, Karen, time to go."

Karen snuggled deeper in the woman's arms. Since the social worker, to their dismay, did nothing to persuade Karen to go with them, they saw no point in remaining at the hospital any longer that day. Dorothy said abruptly, "Karen, honey, we'll be back tomorrow." They waved good-bye as they left.

The next morning the DeBolts found Karen and the social worker waiting for them. They sat in separate chairs: perhaps the social worker now realized what had to be done.

Karen was huddled in her chair. Her expressive eyes were hostile. Bob said, "Let's go for a drive and lunch and a good time."

"I don't want to go out," Karen said.

Dorothy said, "We are going out, Karen." Her voice was calm, soft, but matter-of-fact.

Karen began weeping. "I'm not going. I don't want to!"

Bob pick her up and Dorothy scooped up some toys that were on a chair.

Karen cried, shrieked, yelled, "I don't want to go," and called for the social worker to rescue her. The woman didn't move, and Dorothy was grateful to her.

It was about 150 feet to the car in the parking lot. Karen wept every foot of it. She pushed against Bob's chest with her stumps, struggling to break out of his arms. He was surprised by her strength.

Bob sat Karen in the front seat of their rented car between Dorothy and himself. Dorothy began talking idly—about buildings on the skyline, passing trucks, children on a street corner. In five minutes Karen stopped crying. She wasn't smiling or participating, but she showed no obvious fear.

Bob carried her into the motel room. She sat on the floor and looked around. "Where's my brothers and sisters?" she asked.

"They're at home," Dorothy answered.

"This isn't it?"

"No, dear. Our house and all your brothers and sisters are a long way off. We have to go to the airport and get on an airplane and take a long ride."

It was a new scene for Karen. She didn't know that a king-sized bed was a bed. She asked what "that" was in the kitchenette.

"That's a stove," Dorothy said. "It's used to cook food on."

For most of the afternoon she was content to watch television. The DeBolts did not try to force conversation. They were satisfied to see her relax with them away from the hospital.

Bob sprawled out on the floor near her, commenting occasionally about the cartoons. Then he said, "Say, Karen, I think I'll go out and get something for us to eat. What would you like to have?"

"Potato chips," came the prompt answer.

"Okay," he said, rising. "You got it. And fried chicken?"

"Yeah," Karen said, looking directly into his eyes.

"And Coke?"

"Oh, yeah."

"Can you handle those things without your hooks?"

"Yes."

Toward the end of the afternoon Dorothy wondered why Karen had not wanted to go to the toilet. She asked about it. Karen said, "I did it."

They unbuckled her lowers. She had wet her pants

and her bucket. Dorothy dressed Karen in a pair of her own underpants, washed and dried the bucket, washed the child's underpants, and hung them to dry in the bathroom.

Dorothy held her in her lap for a while, the first time she had held the child without the lowers. It gave her a strange feeling to hold a body without legs hanging down from her lap. As Bob watched the child, an image came to his mind: the figure of a legless middle-aged man on a board with roller-skate wheels under it, extending a handful of pencils toward passersby. Ashamed, he shook his head to erase it.

In midafternoon the talk and shouts of children returning from school filtered into the room. Karen asked Dorothy to hold her so she could look out the window. Dorothy picked her up and sat her on the window sill. The children on the street could have an easy view of the window; Dorothy impulsively wrapped her arms around Karen to hide the view of the child's stumps.

The spontaneous act made her think. She couldn't keep doing that. She couldn't infect Karen with that attitude. The reality had to be accepted. Stumps of arms were stumps. No legs were no legs. Able-bodied children could be cruel. They could laugh and deride. Karen had to be prepared for this, to learn to handle it without losing pride and dignity. The family had a job to do with Karen.

One member of the family started the job for them. Stephanie, twenty-one, was working in upstate New York and arranged to come down to the city to see her new sister. To Bob and Dorothy, it was wonderful to see Steffi bounce in. And Karen seemed to respond the same way. Steffi was a natural with children—the best of all the girls in that respect, in Bob's opinion—and she just moved right in on Karen. She found some music on television, picked the child up, and started dancing with her—wild, exaggerated dancing, swinging the little girl around. Karen was hysterical with laughter.

On the eve of their departure for California, Dorothy and Bob slept restlessly. They awoke early. On the way to the hospital Dorothy told Bob, "You know, honey, this is weird. I feel as if you're driving me to the hospital to have a baby."

"I am. This is no different, except that you haven't been lugging around a body inside you for nine months."

"Nine months. Say, that's funny. While you were showering, I was looking over the correspondence from Spence-Chapin. That first letter from Mrs. Edwards about Karen was dated January 24. Today is October 29. Just about nine months."

At the hospital at least a dozen men and women who had been involved in Karen's care were waiting in the lobby to bid her farewell. The separation was as hard for them as it was for her: she had had love in that hospital from everyone from Sister Theresa, the chief of administration, to Mr. Smith, the sixty-two-year-old maintenance man. Karen was Mr. Smith's favorite child in the entire hospital. He had met her one night when he was walking down the hall. She had scooted in front of him—riding her bottom—on her way to a drink of water. He had carried her back to her room—and been hers from then on. He knew she loved potato chips and he used to slip her bags of them. And when she left, he didn't forget her: for her first Christmas in California, she was greeted by a big, carefully wrapped box, marked "Merry Christmas from the potato-chip man." Inside were some fifty bags of chips.

But now it was time for the hospital members to say good-bye, and they had to do it without upsetting Karen. A quick, "Bye-bye, Karen." A quick kiss on the cheek. Then, a withdrawing and a turning away to hide their tears. Karen's eyes showed confusion and a flashing indecision about whether to cry. She decided against it.

The cab driver who took them to Kennedy Airport was black. Bob felt exhilarated, glad to be free of social workers and the hospital, glad to be going home, and he was amused by the cab driver's continual glancing into his rear-view mirror at them. He obviously couldn't figure out this trio—a blonde woman, a gray-haired white man, and a very black child who wore hooks for hands and carried crutches. Bob put his arm around Karen's shoulder and began a line of chatter: "Karen, did you tell your Mommy what your favorite colors are? . . . Karen, tell Mommy. . . ."

The cab driver couldn't stand it. "Is *she* your daughter?" he asked.

"That's right," Bob said quietly. "Do you think she looks like me or her mother?"

The driver smiled uneasily.

At the airlines terminal as Bob paid the fare he said to the driver, "I was having some fun with you. But she *is* our daughter. We just adopted her."

"No fooling!" the driver said, and drove off grinning.

seven

Bob CARRIED KAREN from his car, up the front porch steps to the door. Dorothy opened it. Bob placed Karen on the threshold step. He wanted to give her the chance to walk into her home. The only barrier to her entering the house was a ¾-inch doorsill. There seemed to be an unspoken agreement among all members of the family who were standing to welcome her in a smiling group on the front porch: Karen was going to take that step into the house on her own.

She leaned her left shoulder against the door jamb for balance. She moved her right crutch over the sill. After sliding her shoulder forward about an inch, she raised her left crutch and moved it across the sill. Then she tried to drag her feet over it. She couldn't. She broke into a sweat. She wore an uneasy, fixed smile. She swiveled in her bucket and simultaneously pushed upward on her crutches. Several children began urging her with, "Come on, Karen, come on," and "You can do it—a little more!" Dorothy couldn't breathe.

Karen hunched a little, pushed again, and dragged her feet to the other side of the threshold. The children cheered. Karen's black skin was gleaming with sweat, and her eyes were bright with pride.

The children had been repeatedly told that Karen had no arms or legs, but Sunee could not picture the disabilities. Dorothy and Bob decided it was best to answer her curiosity immediately, and that first night Sunee came into Noël's bedroom to watch Karen prepare for bed.

Karen was quiet, but didn't seem embarrassed. She slowly removed her prostheses.

Sunee stared at her. "You know what, Karen? God forgot to give you legs."

Karen looked at Sunee's crutches and braces.

Sunee understood. "He remembered to give me mine, but He didn't know they weren't going to work."

Dorothy's and Bob's special gift to Sunee—a sister her own age—was anything but a success at first. Sunee had been prepared for the new member of the family, had seemed happy about having a playmate and companion. But when Karen became a reality in the household, Sunee saw her as a threat, a competitor for her parents' love and time. Sunee almost immediately grew subdued. She began crying without apparent cause. On the morning of Karen's second day in the house, Sunee yelled loudly for Dorothy to help her get on her shoes. Dorothy scolded her and the child again broke into tears.

"Oh, Sunee, this isn't like you," Dorothy said. "You're making a fuss over nothing."

"You're mad at me," Sunee sobbed.

"Honey, I'm not. Honestly." She took the child into her arms.

Karen, too, was reacting to the new situation. Her bed was wet for the second successive morning.

106

That afternoon, after Sunee returned from school, the two girls got into a fight playing Go Fish. Both girls had strong competitive spirits, and they were bickering now about who was going to get first chance at the purple fish with the highest value of ten.

Dorothy said, "Hey, let's quit that and try some other game."

"I don't want to play anything else," Karen decided.

"I don't, either," said Sunee, and she moved away to play with her Barbie dolls.

Later Karen "accidentally" spilled orange juice over Sunee, which sent Sunee into tears.

That evening Melanie told Dorothy, "Sunee said she doesn't like it here anymore. She doesn't want to live here."

"Ever hear of sibling rivalry?" Dorothy asked. "Jealousy. She thinks Karen is going to replace her."

"That's silly."

"But it's real for a child who's feeling it."

In the family room the following afternoon Sunee pushed Karen, knocking her to the floor. "Hey! Whaddya do that for?" Karen demanded.

"You're in my way," Sunee answered.

Dorothy heard the fall. She came in to help Karen to her feet and saw the expression on Sunee's face. "Sunee, please come into the living room for a minute." She sat on the couch and took the child into her arms. Sunee began crying. "Oh, Sunee, I love you," Dorothy said.

Silence.

"Do you love me?"

"Yes."

"Well, I keep loving you more and more. The longer we're together the more I love you."

"What about Karen?"

"I love her too. The same as I love all my children. But nothing can take away my love for you. Nothing. It's going to just keep growing. Forever and ever. Can you believe that?"

Sunee nodded. She stopped sobbing. Dorothy held her in silence. Then Sunee said, "I just heard Trang bring up the laundry basket. I'll tell Karen it's time for us to fold the laundry."

"Thank you, honey," Dorothy said, and lowered her to the floor.

Karen had been wetting her bed every night for three weeks. On the twenty-second night Bob went into her bedroom to kiss her goodnight. Karen was in bed, her prostheses on the floor. Bob sat on the edge of the bed, leaning on his elbow, his other hand on one of her stumps. He said, "Have a good night, Karen. I sure am glad you're my little girl."

Karen said nothing, then suddenly turned and pushed herself erect. Bob sat up. She locked his eyes into her stare. She extended both her stumps, as if presenting evidence, and demanded fiercely, "Why you want me?"

"Why, because I love you." He grasped the stumps in his hands and kissed one, then the other. He looked into her eyes. "Because I love you."

She lowered her eyes, then suddenly toppled into his arms. He held her closely. Neither said anything. Then Bob lowered her to the pillow. She again stared into his eyes as Bob took her face between his hands and kissed her cheeks. "I love you," he said. "Good night, sweetheart."

Right: Anh and Sunee climbing the stairs.

Below: Tich is fitted for new braces by a prosthetics technician as Dorothy looks on (1970).

Bottom: The old braces stand empty as Tich tries on the new.

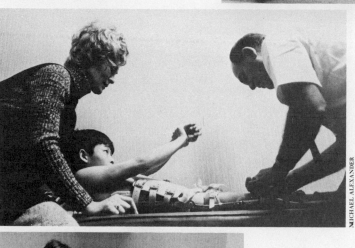

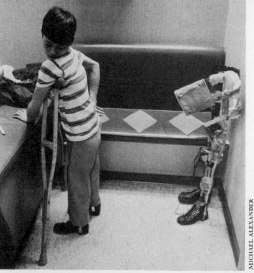

ANDERS-STERN

MICHAEL ALEXANDER

MICHAEL ALEXANDER

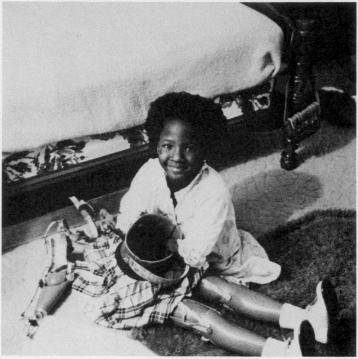

ANDERS-STERN

Karen is about to put herself back together again.

Opposite: A little heat in the kitchen: Sunee and Karen.

Mimi and Karen.

Below: Blind Wendy is welcomed to the family. Clockwise from Wendy: Sunee, Karen, Trang, Anh (partially obscured), Melanie, Stephanie, Tich, Dat (behind him, a visiting friend), Dorothy, and Bob.

ANDERS-STERN

COURTESY SAN FRANCISCO EXAMINER

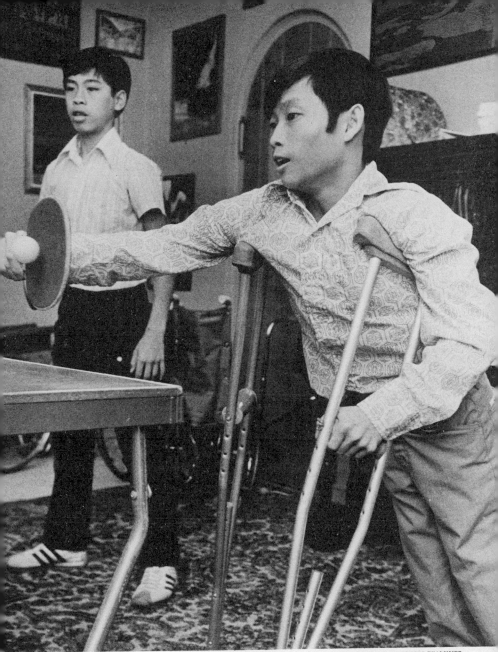

Trang and Tich.

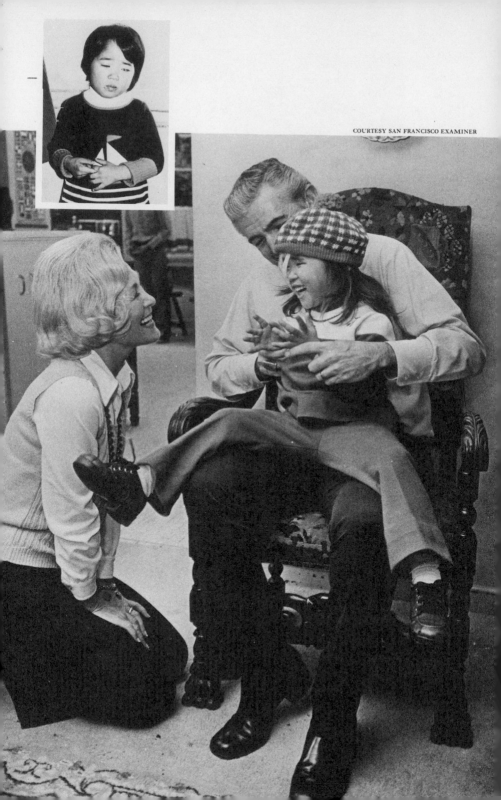

COURTESY SAN FRANCISCO EXAMINER

Opposite, inset: Before her adoption, Wendy was known in the Korean orphanage as "the girl who never smiles."

Opposite: Wendy can see! Dorothy and Bob have just brought her home from the hospital after the corneal transplant.

Phong pitches to Karen in the backyard while Sunee awaits her turn at bat.

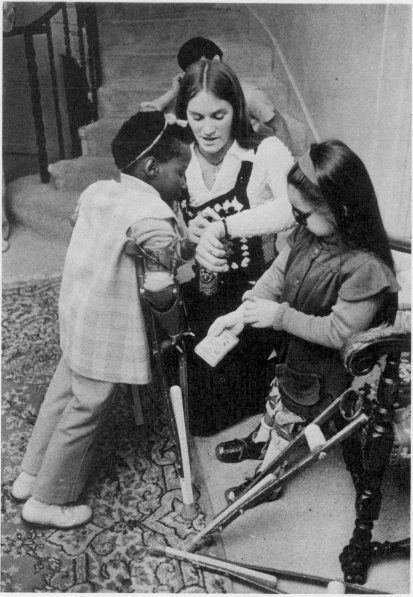

Above: Sunee, Wendy, and Karen always find Dorothy's accordion fascinating.

Opposite: Noël teaches Karen to tell time. Sunee, in dark glasses, is pretending to be a movie star.

Below: Wendy sorts and folds the laundry in the basement room.

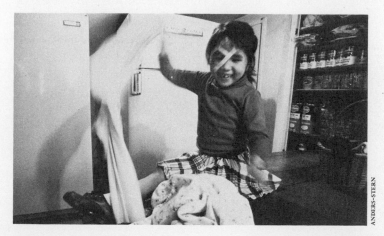

Still staring at him, Karen slowly extended her stumps to touch his wrists, softly, tenderly.

Bob slowly rose from the bed and went to his bedroom. He cried the tears held back in Karen's room.

The next morning Karen was dry; she did not wet her bed thereafter.

At the hospital Karen had been looking forward to the annual Halloween party. To soften her disappointment at not being there for it, Bob and Dorothy had promised her a Halloween evening of her own, trick-or-treating in the neighborhood. It would be a first for Karen, a new adventure, and she made the DeBolts repeat the promise.

When the day came Dorothy improvised costumes for Karen and Sunee. Karen was wearing a dress, and her artificial legs and braces were obvious. She had wanted to wear pants to conceal her prostheses, but Dorothy told her, "Look, honey. There's no sense in hiding them. We all know you have them. Sometimes you wear pants and sometimes a dress, whichever is right at that time. But you have nothing to hide. Be proud of how well you do on those legs."

Dat pushed Sunee in her wheelchair, and Bob pushed Karen.

At the first house a woman answered the bell, handed the two girls bags of candy, and chatted with Bob for a minute. To the side of the door was a window with the conventional hollowed-out pumpkin on the sill. A candle, too large for the pumpkin, was burning in the interior. The heat had melted away some of the pumpkin, and the mouth was sagging. The woman nodded toward it and said, "You'll have to excuse that pumpkin. Looks as if it has a cleft palate. I'd better get rid of it."

"Please don't say that too loud," Bob said. "If Dorothy hears about it, she'll come over and adopt it."

At the third house, a woman looked in surprise at the girls, handed Sunee two bags of candy, and said, "Give one to the other little girl."

Bob said, "Sunee, let your sister take her own candy. That's part of the fun."

As Karen reached out with her hooks, the woman extended the bag and, at the same time, drew back a little. At four or five houses, the reaction was the same. Surprise. Offense. Revulsion. Some neighbors really didn't want to be confronted by two such children.

Back out on the street Dat was livid. "We ought to go back later and punch those people in the mouth," he told Bob.

"Cool it," Bob advised. "Those people don't count." He was glad that both the girls, who were more interested in the candy, had missed the reactions. Later, at home, Bob told Dorothy, "It seems that some of our neighbors aren't exactly delighted to see our little black kid poking her claws toward them."

"Too bad," Dorothy said. "You brought some of the problems of the world to their doors. They don't want to know about the problems. But I still think some of the reaction comes from ignorance. They just don't know how beautiful these kids are."

But months later, Bob learned a lesson. He was lifting Karen into the small yellow school bus that took her to the Whitton School for the Orthopedically Handicapped when he was shocked by a small boy, apparently a cerebral palsy victim, in the rear seat. The child wore a helmet. His eyes were blazing and his face was contorted and his mouth twisted as if he were being tortured on the rack. His hands curled stiffly toward his wrists like frozen claws. Bob found he wanted the sight not to exist. After the bus drew away he stood on the sidewalk for a few minutes.

Then he went into the house and told Dorothy about his experience and feelings. "Who am I to criticize the neighbors? I react no differently."

"You were taken by surprise, just as they were. You know that you'd feel differently about that boy after spending an hour with him. The people around here who were taken aback by Karen would also change after some contact with her."

Information about Karen quickly sifted through the community and Bob's company. Three days after Karen's arrival, Dorothy received a call from an acquaintance. "Say, the news about your adopting Karen has really spread," the woman reported.

"Great, great," Dorothy said. "If only more people would do what we've done."

"Well, it's not exactly that kind of reaction."

"I don't follow."

"I heard three comments. One woman believes you're exploiting these kids in some way. Another wondered if you were just doing this to prove your racial tolerance. The third said the kids would have been better off where they were originally."

"Did she mean in a hospital or an orphanage?"

"I guess so."

"What do you think about our adopting Karen?"

"Well, I think it's kind of your business."

An hour later the phone rang and a woman's voice said, "I have a call for Mrs. N. Lover—"

120

Dorothy was about to interrupt and tell her that she had a wrong number.

"—N as in nigger."

Dorothy was momentarily shocked, then said, "Yes, this is she. What can I do for you?" There was a click at the other end of the line. In a short time another woman called—Dorothy was sure that this one was well intentioned—and asked if the family also took in abandoned animals.

She sat for a while staring through the bedroom window at the plum trees in the backyard. She was neither angered or revolted, but overcome with a sense of melancholy that subdued her for the rest of the day. That evening she told Bob about the calls and asked him what kind of feedback he'd had at his office.

"It's been a rotten day," Bob said, slumping into a chair. "I feel awfully disappointed, and I know I shouldn't. I'm not trying to be a hero. But the reaction sure made me feel lousy. You know, we have this Affirmative Action Program—we're supposed to employ eleven percent from minority groups. It's a union problem rather than a contractor's responsibility. The hard hats and section chiefs oppose it, but I've fought for it.

"Well, I was out checking one section of the project today and the field superintendent came up to me and said, 'One thing I can say for you is that you're helping our Affirmative Action Program.' I asked him what he meant. He said, 'The more in-house coons we have the better off we are.' The construction industry makes rough fun, but I never expected this. I told him, 'Look, you son of a bitch, whatever you do in your personal life is your business, and I don't butt in. So you stay the hell out of my affairs. I don't want to hear what you have to say because whatever you have to say isn't worth a shit.' He'll never butt into my personal life again!

"Nobody else in the office said a word. I think they all know about Karen. The fact that they're ignoring the adoption tells me pretty much what they think. But it doesn't matter a damn to me what they think."

A few weeks later Dorothy took Sunee and Karen to the orthopedic surgeon for an examination. On the way home she stopped at a Piedmont grocery store for a few items and left the girls in the car. On her return a woman, who appeared to be in her seventies, stood by the car, looking at the girls. She asked Dorothy, "Are you Mrs. DeBolt?"

"Yes." She was defensive, prepared for an insulting comment.

The stranger moved to her, put her arms around her, and exclaimed, "You make me proud to be a woman!"

There were other positive reactions, so many that it turned out it was Karen's arrival that gave birth to the idea of the DeBolts' organization of AASK. During Karen's first weeks at home, they received several dozen letters from people who had read about the adoption, people asking how they too could adopt a handicapped child. Bob and Dorothy could do nothing but refer them to agencies. But they kept thinking about it. There should be some service that would have a record of disabled children, the so-called "unadoptables," and of adults willing to take these children—a service that could be the channel between children and potential parents.

Life in a house with a family was an adventure for six-year-old Karen, and her excitement and astonishment over the mundane and routine aspects of living were delights to Dorothy and Bob. She was fascinated by the contents of the refrigerator and the kitchen cabinet drawers. She had never seen anyone cook dinner, never been wheeled in a shopping cart through a supermarket, never been in a theater. She had never before seen the countryside—rolling hills, a herd of cows, a girl riding a horse. She had never witnessed any display of adult affection: she was obviously intrigued by the open and spontaneous affection between her parents. Bob and Dorothy had never hesitated to embrace and kiss in front of the children if they felt like it.

The DeBolts immediately set out to help Karen become as independent as possible, but they didn't have to push hard. She was eager to meet every challenge, to do what the able-bodied could do. She soon began "feeling" with her steel hooks and other prostheses by transferring sensations tested on her cheeks or recognized visually. "Ouch, that water is hot." "Yup-Yup's coat feels soft"—she was no longer afraid of the dog. "I better put on warmer pants." "Sunee, your hair is so nice and soft."

One day Karen and Sunee were playing on the porch with Yup-Yup, and they asked Dorothy to put the dog's chain on Karen's hook so she could hold and pet the animal. Dorothy did so and went back to work at her desk in the bedroom when she suddenly heard great shrieks. She looked out and there was Karen lying on her back on the cement porch—both her arms off. When Dorothy reached her, Karen was laughing uproariously as she explained that Yup-Yup's chain had gotten caught in her hook. Dorothy looked around— and there was the dog running down the walk with

Karen's arms. And Dorothy stood there yelling, "Come back with Karen's arms!"—and wondering what the neighbors thought went on around there.

At the hospital Karen had used a fork and spoon with handles that were curled to make them easier to hold between her hooks. The DeBolts had left them at the hospital, convinced that Karen could learn to use conventional utensils.

The two hooks on each hand were lined with smooth rubber and held closed by a heavy rubber band. Karen could open the hooks by moving her shoulder, pulling a cable that separated the two prongs of each hook. She eagerly tried to use the household's utensils, but her effort sent knife, fork, and food flying across the table: the handles kept slipping between the hooks. Bob solved that problem by lining Karen's utensils with heavy abrasive tape, the kind used on the floors of industrial plants to prevent slips on spilled oil. The tape increased friction, enabling Karen to control firmly the angle of her knife and fork. She had never used a knife at the hospital—an aide had always cut up her food—and it took her several weeks to acquire the knack as she went from cutting a fried egg to vegetables, then hamburger and firm meats.

Her skill with the hooks increased virtually every day. Her drawing and writing improved. She peeled hard-boiled eggs and oranges. She learned to hold a slice of hard-boiled egg so precisely that her hooks neither allowed the slice to fall nor squashed the delicate yolk. After one failure she could hold an ice cream cone without cracking the fragile cone.

She loved to help Dorothy in the kitchen. "Karen, would you give me a hand with the potato salad?"

"Sure, Mom."

124

"Now, look, dear, this gadget is called a potato peeler. Watch me. See how it peels that skin right off."

No toy could have given Karen more joy.

She also learned how to help with the preparations for an omelet. Dorothy cracked an egg on the edge of the bowl and dropped the contents into the bowl. Karen tried it. On her first attempts she squeezed the egg too hard and both egg and pieces of shell fell into the bowl. Then she held the egg too loosely and it slipped from between the hooks and broke on the counter. Finally she got it right—the correct pressure to retain the egg and the correct force to crack it. Then she pulled apart the shell and dropped the contents into the bowl. After finishing all the eggs with great concentration, she looked up at Dorothy, a broad smile on her face. Dorothy hugged her.

Karen became so adept with her hooks that the other members of the family lost sight of the fact that they were not hands. When Sunee and Melanie wet their fingers to pick up cake and cookie crumbs, Karen automatically ran her tongue over her hooks so that the crumbs would adhere to them. Once Sunee swung swiftly toward Karen after Karen had accidentally slammed a door on her hooks. "Does it hurt?" Sunee asked with deep concern. "Is it bleeding?" The two girls looked at each other for a moment, then began laughing.

One afternoon Sunee was on the floor with her braces off. As a lark she placed her useless legs in the split position and tried to balance herself.

Dorothy saw Karen's eyes as she watched, and she said quickly, "You'd better not try it with your prostheses, Karen, because you could wreck them."

"Karen can do it when she takes them off," Sunee suggested.

"That's fine, Sunee, but what is she going to split?"

Both girls found that very funny.

Karen was faced with three big problems: how to get off the floor, how to climb the staircase as Sunee did, and how to go to the toilet on her own. She grimly accepted the need to be lifted when she fell and to be carried up and down the stairs—and she was always polite with a "thank you"—but she resented her dependence. Karen did not mind being helped to use the toilet if someone offered, "Do you need to go?" She didn't like asking for that help, however, and she would rather wet her bucket than ask.

About two weeks after she first came, Karen fell near the bed in the first-floor bedroom. She sat there, laughing at her mishap and Dorothy laughed with her. Then she tried to get upright. She managed to get her hooks on the mattress to pull herself up, but the hooks kept slipping. Her legs kept folding at the hips. The situation lost its humor. Her mouth was set. Her eyes seemed to steam with determination.

Dorothy stood by. She knew she must not reach down and pick the child up. Tich and Anh, in the kitchen, heard the clanging of braces and grunts. They swung into the bedroom and stood there reviewing the situation. Bob joined them. None of the onlookers could suggest a way for Karen to get to her feet. She kept trying—and her artificial legs kept collapsing. The sweat dripped from her face.

Tears came to her eyes, her way of announcing that she had temporarily given up, and Bob lifted her from the floor, murmuring words of comfort: "You'll get it, Karen, you'll find a way to do it." Then Dorothy

held her. Karen stopped crying. Dorothy was overcome: even in despair Karen did not lose her pride; even
then she held her neck in a regal manner.

The following afternoon, Karen told her mother, "I
want to walk up the stairs."

Dorothy looked at her in surprise.

"Everybody goes up the stairs except me."

"Okay. Fine. Let's go."

The first step of the staircase was wider than the
others, and the wrought-iron balustrade curved con-
cavely toward it. Dorothy lifted Karen to the second
step. The child put her left arm over the banister, trying to pull herself by pulling with that arm and pushing
against the right crutch with her other hooks. She
couldn't do it, couldn't get enough leverage with her left
hooks.

After a dozen or so failures she stopped to catch
her breath and to consider the problem. "Maybe I can
go *down* the stairs, backwards."

"It's worth a try," Dorothy said. "I'll be right behind so you don't have anything to worry about if you
slip." She lifted Karen to the third step.

Karen swung her left arm and prosthesis over the
railing and grasped a baluster with her hooks. She lowered the right crutch to the step below her. By swiveling her bucket she forced her shoes backward toward
the edge of the step. She could see her heels go over the
edge. At the moment the toes of the shoes slipped off
the step, she released her grip and grabbed for the next
lower baluster to prevent herself from falling.

She missed and fell into Dorothy's arms. Again
and again and again she tried. Sometimes she succeeded
in catching the baluster, but her legs failed to land in
the right position and they buckled at the knees. At

127

other times she couldn't get the right crutch to the step below her: all her weight was on the one crutch and she couldn't lift it to another position.

Karen struggled for twenty minutes or so until Dorothy said, "That's enough for today, honey. We'll give it another try tomorrow. Nobody got it on the first try. It took Sunee quite a while. You'll do it."

Each day they worked on the steps when the other children were in school and Bob was at his office. Sometimes Karen concentrated so hard on changing balusters with her left hooks that she forgot about the right crutch, which left her grasp and went flying down the stairs. But she never quit. It was only when Dorothy saw the tears of frustration in the child's eyes that she said, "Okay, Karen, enough for today. We'll tackle it again tomorrow."

Once, after holding Karen for a minute—the child was breathing like a steam engine—Dorothy walked into the kitchen, muttering, "Come on, God, knock it off. Let the poor little kid make it."

On December 20, Karen perfectly coordinated the swiveling of her shoes, the movement of the crutch, and the changing of position of her hooks. She dropped to the step below without losing her balance.

Dorothy was all set to catch her as she had done scores of times before. Karen stood there like a statue. "Karen!" Dorothy shouted. Karen said nothing but her eyes shone. Dorothy said, "You did it! You learned how to do it. Let's not tell Daddy. It's five days till Christmas. Let's see how many steps you can do in that time. Then surprise him."

The next day Karen failed on the steps. Nothing worked. The crutch wouldn't slide back. She couldn't release the hook from the baluster at precisely the right moment, and she yanked so hard that she pulled the prosthesis off her stump. She tried again and again, Dorothy praising and encouraging, but the harder she struggled, the more extreme was her failure. Dorothy finally told her to stop. On the following day, December 23, everything synchronized again—and Karen descended five steps without a fall.

About noon on Christmas, after all the gifts had been opened, Dorothy told Bob, "Karen has something special for you for Christmas. If you'll go to the top of the stairs she'll give it to you."

Bob ran to the second-floor landing. Dorothy carried Karen to the top step and stood about five steps below her. Karen lowered her head. She got her hooks around the baluster, dropped one crutch out of her way, and established the other on the step below her. She began the swiveling motion with her hips, moving her shoes back to the edge of the step. She dropped to the step below her. Then another step, and another, until she had climbed down five steps and stood directly before Dorothy. Then, for the first time during her precarious journey, she looked up at Bob and in her low, husky voice said, "Merry Christmas, Daddy."

Bob's cheeks were wet as he ran down the steps and grabbed her. "Karen, Karen! I've never been given a Christmas gift so valuable in my life!" He clutched the child to him and then, with one arm, included Dorothy in the embrace. They held each other in silence.

That entire Christmas period had been special. Karen's beloved Stephanie—Steffi—had come home in December and had put Karen and Sunee to work making gingerbread men: making designs, using the cookie cutter, choosing food coloring, and so on. And Dorothy had the satisfaction of watching the daughter she had taught to do this teach the new children in the family.

They used handmade ornaments and popcorn strings for the tree and decorated it themselves. It was top-heavy and lopsided, but it was all done by the children: papier-mâché creations, some good, some terrible, some falling apart. The lower branches were sagging with a colorful jumble of ornaments put there every whichway by the younger children. Once when Karen dropped her crutch and tried to pick it up, she fell into the tree bringing dozens of decorations down with her, and all had to be rehung.

Bob's daughter Doni, who lived with his former wife in New Mexico, was there, and Bob's parents, Nana and Poppy, came carrying enough boxes of presents to fill the hall. It was the first time they had met Karen, and, after they recovered from their first uneasiness, they were delighted with her. Bob's parents filled a special need for Dorothy: her own parents were dead, and she felt blessed to have these.

On Christmas morning they could hardly find the tree for the presents. Each child had made a gift for everyone else in the family: opening them took two and a half hours. From Anh came a marvelous oil painting, knitted elves' hats for Sunee and Karen, macrame belts for the older girls. Tich had made candles and cut-glass designs. Trang had made trivets and a wall shelf in woodworking class. There were sketches and wood prints by Dat and Trang. Melanie, who was just learning to sew, had made a shirt for Doni and a matching one for herself; both girls wore them. Steffi had a fireplace poker she had blacksmithed and some pewter spoons she had made; and she had made aprons for the little girls. Mimi had brought each person a different kind of plant—each in a pot she had painted and decorated herself. Noël had written in Old English script the verse now on the kitchen bulletin board. Doni had made a beautiful God's eye of yarn, which became the decoration for the top of the tree. Mike and Marty sent a long Christmas tape they recorded in Hawaii. But there was no word from Kim.

When Bob and Dorothy finally got upstairs that night, Dorothy found that Bob had written her a message on the little blackboard in their dressing room: "You are my Christmas. Thank you, God. End of a very special Christmas day."

By early January 1973 Karen was able to descend the entire staircase backward. Then she set out once more to climb up the stairs, as everybody else did. The other children told Dorothy and Bob that they'd take care of helping and protecting her. Sunee tried to explain how she mounted the steps. Anh displayed his technique. Tich had always found it easier to go up the stairs backward, but Karen declined to try that method. She wanted to climb forward. Dat and Trang spent many after-school hours helping and encouraging the child.

On a Monday evening in January, Trang called to Dorothy on the second floor and asked in an easy tone, "Mom, did you see what Karen can do?"

"No," Dorothy said. She heard Karen giggle.

Dorothy stood at the second-floor landing. Karen looked up at her from the second step. The child placed her elbow and hooks on the banister, grasping the railing, not a baluster. She put her chin on the railing to increase support and balance. She moved the right crutch to the next step. Then, pulling on the railing and pushing against the crutch, she heaved herself to the next step. No one stood beside her. No one was behind her. Twelve-year-old Trang watched from the foyer. Slowly and confidently she lurched up the nineteen steps until she reached Dorothy, who was on her knees with outstretched arms. It was January 15, Martin Luther King, Jr.'s, birthday, and the words "We shall overcome" came to Dorothy's mind.

A few days later Karen was working on the steep flight of ten steps from the kitchen to the basement. She slipped on the first step, lost her hold on the banister, and fell. She screamed as her body slammed down the steps. Dorothy had been in the kitchen and ran down the steps. Karen lay sprawled on the concrete floor, wailing in pain. Blood ran from her nose, upper lip, forehead, and bitten tongue. Her artificial left arm had been torn off her stump and the hooks had gouged her left side.

Dorothy carried her upstairs and dressed her cuts and bruises. She called Bob home from work, and they sat with Karen. They were concerned about a possible skull fracture or concussion, and they watched for signs of vomiting, listlessness, or drowsiness. But the injuries were apparently superficial, and soon Karen was asking if she could play with Sunee.

Dorothy later thought about the accident and shivered. "Can you imagine the terror and helplessness that kid must have felt?" she asked Bob. "To go backward down those stairs? Falling. Flying. No way to stop herself."

Thereafter Karen was very cautious on the basement stairs. She practiced for several weeks, an older child always with her, until she gained sureness and proficiency.

Although she had stopped wetting her bed a few

weeks after joining the family, Karen continued to wet her bucket during the day—because she continued to be reluctant to ask to be taken to the toilet. The urine was rusting the metal parts and rotting the plastic of her bucket. At each wetting the bucket had to be soaped, rinsed several times, and dried. Bob and Dorothy repeatedly explained the problem to Karen and told her to ask for help but she continued to wet. They punished her by restricting her to her room while the other children played in the family room.

After several confinements and scoldings, Karen began asking for help. Dorothy praised her lavishly the first time she did. Whoever took her to the bathroom had to remove her lowers and sit her on the edge of the toilet: she balanced by holding onto the water tank. The other kids were always ready to help—doing things for Karen was fun. Once when Melanie had taken her, she said, "Hey, Karen, while your legs are off I have an idea." She ran into the kitchen for a shopping bag. She ran back and inserted Karen into the bag. Only her head showed. Then Melanie marched with the bag from room to room, proclaiming, "Look what I bought at Safeway. They were having a big special on them today." Karen's laughter rang through the house.

After several weeks Karen was routinely making requests to be taken to the toilet, and it didn't matter to her whether her assistance came from a female or a male. One afternoon Dorothy heard a commotion in the first-floor bathroom and ran to it. Anh was supporting himself on one crutch, his back against the toilet tank to maintain his balance. His weight also was on the tank lever, causing a slight flow of water. He was leaning down into the bowl, his left hand under Karen's armpit, grimly trying to pull her out. Only her head and neck showed above the seat. She was staring desperately up at Anh, yelling, "Don't flush, don't flush!" The scene was so unexpected and unimaginable that Dorothy burst into laughter. As she pulled Karen out of the bowl Anh admonishingly said, "Not so funny to fall in toilet."

The next day Bob brought home an infant's-sized plastic toilet seat that fitted over the conventional seat.

It took many months, but Karen passed another obstacle. She learned to pull herself erect from a sitting position on the floor. Then Bob asked Dorothy, "When do we start working on Karen to go to the toilet on her own? I know it's going to take one hell of an effort on her part. But she can't always have someone take her. So when does she start learning? Now, when she's seven? Or at twelve? Seventeen?"

"We do it now," said Dorothy. "For her sake, right now."

They tentatively, gently, proposed the challenge to Karen. She didn't respond.

"Let's talk about it tomorrow," Bob suggested. The child said nothing.

The next day Bob sat her on his lap and said, "Let's make it a game, Karen. Let's make believe you're alone. You have to go. You can't do it in your bucket. Big girls don't do that. You have to use the toilet on your own."

"I can't do it."

"We can figure out a way."

"I can't, Daddy. Somebody has to put me on the seat."

"That one's tough. I've thought about it and talked it over with Mommy. You'll have to do it differently from everybody else."

Karen waited apprehensively.

"What you'll have to do, honey, is lift up the seat, stand on your hooks, hang your little bottom over the edge, and do what you have to do."

Karen began crying.

For months, a solo visit to the toilet was an ordeal for her. Swing into the bathroom. Gather toilet tissue. Drop to the floor. Unstrap and unbuckle the bucket and ease out of it. Remove underpants. Pull body up, position hooks on each side of seat, balance between them, standing on "hands." Use tissue. Get into pants. Squirm into bucket, and redo straps and buckles. Struggle to the upright position. Flush toilet. Wash hooks. Elapsed time: fifteen to twenty minutes.

For several months it was a struggle. Karen shed tears, often joined in sympathy by Sunee. She resisted, and urinated or defecated in her bucket—and was made to clean it. She shoved a chair to the sink, mounted it, soaped and scrubbed the bucket, and rinsed it. It took a year, during which Karen frequently wet her bucket, but she finally reconciled herself to the routine—and passed another major obstacle in the path of her independence. Once they got her to school, however, the DeBolts discovered they would have to educate her overprotective teacher to the fact that this child did not need to be helped to go to the bathroom: it took a demonstration by Karen to prove the point.

It was in mid-January 1973 that Dorothy enrolled Karen in the Whitton School for the Orthopedically Handicapped, where Sunee was attending first grade. While she was there, Dorothy had a conference with Sunee's teacher, who had nothing but praise for the child. She told of Sunee's humor, intelligence, and unconscious leadership: "One day she came into class with a moustache painted on her face. In a little while every kid in the room had a painted moustache." But her main story was how Sunee had worked to make a new child in class comfortable. It was a little girl who spoke only Spanish. For the sake of that child, the teacher had taught all the others a few Spanish phrases, but Sunee was the only child who went to the new girl and used them. And the first English word the new girl said was "Sunee." The two children would sit and talk, each in her own language, but they understood each other. And the teacher reported, "That child learned more from Sunee than from me."

During a recess on that same school visit, Dorothy overheard a girl ask Karen, "Who's that white woman with you?"

"That's no white woman," Karen replied. "That's my mother. I adopted her."

That afternoon Dorothy waited for the school bus to deliver Karen. "How'd things go?"

"All right."

"Anything special happen?"

"It was all new. A lady helped me go to the toilet. A girl was there and she saw me take off my legs. She asked me if I could take myself apart and put myself together again whenever I wanted to. I said, 'Sure, I can.' "

Dorothy laughed. "That's funny."

"It's true," Karen assured her. "I can."

Over the weeks and months Dorothy got written and telephone reports from Karen's young teacher: "Karen was very quiet for the first three or four days and really said nothing. Then she began talking and laughing with some of the kids, but became silent if adults were around. . . ."

"We were trying to find a way for her to use scissors. She had the idea of filling the inside of the handles with clay and leaving an opening just large enough for her hooks. Eventually we hit on the idea of winding a lot of heavy yarn around the handle to reduce the size of the opening. . . ."

"She is very determined. She loves to play baseball and I hold my breath when she's out there. She falls and can't get up on her own. She's worked that out with Charlie. When she falls, she gets her crutches and Charlie raises her by her armpits until she is high enough to squeeze the crutches under her armpits. Then she's ready to play again. Karen is not too afraid to ask for help. When she goes down she says, 'Charlie, pick me up.' She figured out a way to sit down. She stands and I push the chair into the back of her legs and she just falls into it. The aide usually helps her out of the chair and into the upright position. She can't make it on her own. Except yesterday. The children were sitting around a work table. A boy said something Karen didn't like. She pushed her chair back from the table. She was angry and determined. She got up on the crutches on her own. It took a lot of work. She went over to the boy and whacked him on the shoulder with her hooks. . . ."

"Mrs. DeBolt, Karen fell a short while ago and gashed her head and it had to be stitched. She's fine, but we're sending her home. I thought it might make her feel scared and cautious, but it didn't. She's ready to go again. . . ."

"Some children coming into this school need to be taught how to play with other children. But not Karen.

137

She's becoming a leader of some group activities. At play period she'll say, 'All right, let's play baseball,' and a bunch of kids will follow her to the playground. . . ."

"Did Karen tell you about the Walkathon? Fund raising. Each child had a sponsor who paid ten cents for every lap a child made around the school area. It's quite a long walk. Karen did the maximum of ten laps on her crutches. Other kids with bad legs used a wheelchair, but Karen hates the wheelchair. She's a very determined, very competitive little girl. She gets great satisfaction out of doing things on her own."

In early May Karen arrived from school with a book of tickets. "I gotta sell raffle tickets," she explained to Dorothy. "Somebody can win something and we're going to use the money to go on a special trip—our whole class!"

Melanie offered to wheel Karen in her chair from house to house. Dorothy knew that Karen was still ill at ease when first meeting adult strangers, so she helped Karen work out her pattern: "Hi. I'm Karen DeBolt. I'm selling raffle tickets for the Whitton School so that our class can take a trip. I hope you can buy a ticket."

Karen put on a fresh blouse and Dorothy tied ribbons in her hair.

Melanie and Karen returned in a half hour. Karen was crying. "It was awful," Melanie told her mother. "The first five houses were all right. At the next house the woman opened the door and looked at Karen and her hooks. Before Karen could say a word she said, 'I'm busy and I'm not interested,' and she slammed the door on us. Karen got upset. That was a terrible woman."

Dorothy felt the rage rise in her, but she tried to make light of the incident. "Maybe that lady wasn't feeling very well today, Karen, and that's why she wasn't nice. Or maybe she just isn't a nice lady. You're going to find that some people are not nice. Were all the other people nice?"

"Yes."

"See? Most people are nice. You don't have to be mad at the one lady who wasn't nice. Maybe you should just feel sorry for her. . . . You know, darling, not everybody is going to like you. Some people don't like me. They don't like the way I look or they don't like what I say or they don't like what I do. But that's all right. I don't like everybody, either."

Karen nodded. "And I don't like that lady."

Near the end of the school term Dorothy hired a black woman to help her with the housework. Late one morning the woman told her, "Karen and I were talking before I took her out to the school bus. She said that it was going to be Parents' Day at school on Friday, and that her mommy would be there. I explained to her that you weren't her real mommy. She was black and you were white. I didn't want the child to be confused."

"What'd Karen say?" Dorothy asked, without showing her resentment.

"She didn't understand. So I told her again about the difference in skin."

"In this house the real mother is the one who loves the child and takes care of her," Dorothy pointed out. "That's me. As she grows older she'll ask us about birth and race and at that time we'll answer her questions. One mother gave birth to her. That mother is not a part of her life now. Karen's real mother is the one that she's with, the one that she feels good about."

That evening Dorothy sat with Karen alone in her bedroom. She invented an opening: "I ran into an old friend of mine today who has a black girl who looks a lot like you, Karen. The lady has white skin, just like me. Somebody asked this little girl if the lady was her mommy, how come she had white skin and the little girl black skin? The little girl said what does skin have to do with who is your mommy?"

Karen weighed that. "Does that mean you're my real mommy even though you have white skin?"

"Of course. Oh, another mommy bore you, but now you are my little girl, my daughter, forever. It's like with Sunee. Sunee's skin is not like mine and her eyes are not the same shape as mine. But I'm her mommy, right? And she's my daughter, right?"

"Yes."

"Well, another mommy bore Sunee, too. But I'm her real mommy."

Karen inched closer to Dorothy. She extended her right hooks and they held hands.

eight

WHEN THEY got tired of playing baseball, the children had a long discussion about which thing they should do next, between now and lunchtime. This used up just about all the minutes remaining until Phong was to go up to the house and bring down the paper bag with the seven packets of sandwiches and fresh fruit that he'd packed the night before; it was his job to prepare lunches. J.R. took off his shirt because it felt good to get a tan and suggested they rehearse their parts in the play he'd made up. Wendy said she didn't feel like it, and she wandered off to the side of the play area to a patch of daisies. Karen wanted to bounce a basketball, and she asked Wendy to get the ball for her—which Wendy started to do until she remembered she wasn't supposed to wait on Karen. Lee was lying, half dozing, on the picnic table, where she'd been right through the ball game, and Twe sat in one of the swings, barely moving it, her face turned toward the July sun overhead, warm lids shut over blind eyes. No one could agree with anyone else about what they'd do next, and they were finally about to take up J.R.'s suggestion about the play, when Dorothy called from the top of the driveway, "Lunchtime, Phong."

As Phong started out for the house, Wendy shouted to him to bring a glass of water for her daisies. Phong came back carrying the tray with their food and eight cups of water—seven for their lunch and one for the daisies. The daisies were already wilting and they sagged over the edge of the cup, but it didn't matter. Wendy knew her mother would like her present anyway. . . .

There was a photograph on Dorothy's desk that had stood there since May 1969, when she was still a widow. It was a picture of a young Korean child taken in the Holt orphanage in Seoul. An American nurse had written Dorothy that the child was a diabetic and could not get the necessary dietary and medical supervision in the orphanage. The nurse had implored Dorothy to find a home in the States for the child, who was losing weight and lapsing into comas. Dorothy had gotten the assurance of the necessary medical care from the local diabetic association—and she had found a home for the child with a woman in Santa Cruz who had adopted five children already and who shared Dorothy's interest in finding homes for handicapped children. But even though Dorothy stressed the urgency of the care to the Department of Social Welfare, all she got from them was the promise that the request would be processed in due time.

Four months after her first letter the nurse in Korea wrote that the child had lapsed into another coma and died that day.

Dorothy wept in anger at the system that allowed

that child to die. She kept the photograph in front of her as a constant reminder that no child in need must ever be treated as a case number to be "processed in due time." Over the next four years, the nurse and Dorothy had corresponded frequently about Korean handicapped orphans, and Dorothy had been able to find families for eight of those children. Then in late 1971 the nurse mentioned that a Seoul policeman had found a three-and-a-half-year-old blind girl abandoned on the streets. An accompanying photograph showed Kim Kwan Ok to be a small, forlorn-looking child. The nurse added that the girl bore mysterious, patterned burn scars on her body and arms. Dorothy called a dozen families eager to adopt, but none wanted a blind child.

In subsequent correspondence concerning other orphans the nurse referred often to Kim Kwan Ok, who she feared was becoming seriously emotionally damaged. The child became a ward of the Holt Adoption Program, and her photograph was circulated in the United States among families that had inquired about adoptions, but there were no takers.

Then, in July 1973, the nurse wrote that the child had been hospitalized at a Korean army base for the removal of one progressively deteriorating, pain-causing eye. The surgeon thought the remaining eye, which could differentiate between light and dark, might benefit from a corneal transplant; the hospital, however, was not equipped to do one. And the transplant would have to be attempted soon, or the child would be permanently blind.

The news nagged Dorothy. After a sleepless night, she told Bob, "This thing with the blind kid is driving me nuts. How can we leave her there, knowing she is going to be permanently blind? How can we leave her there, knowing she stands a chance here—if we act fast?"

Bob said, "Then let's get moving on it."

After initiating the adoption with Holt, Dorothy called the Adoption Services Section of the Department of Health and talked with the assistant chief, explaining the emergency situation. He responded immediately by assigning the case to a social worker, who did the home study promptly, efficiently, and sympathetically. When the report approving the DeBolts as an adoptive family was completed, Bob sent Holt Adoption Program a check for $1,060 to cover the $185 for the child's transportation and the $875 for processing. A check for $100 was also sent to the Department of Health to cover the cost of the home study. All costs of the medical and surgical care for the child would be paid by the Crippled Children's Services, a state agency. While trying to accelerate the completion of the paperwork, Dorothy was making inquiries to find a surgeon known for his skill in pediatric corneal transplants.

Before the social worker's first visit, Dorothy told Sunee and Karen that they would soon have a new five-year-old sister. "She's in Korea now, just like you were, Sunee. Her first name is Kwan, but Dad and I have decided to call her Wendy."

Sunee said, "She can use my crutches."

"That's kind of you, but she won't need them."

"Does she have legs?" Karen asked.

"Yes, she does."

Sunee said, "And they work?"

"They work all right, but her eyes don't work," Dorothy explained.

"Well, if Sunee can use my crutches," Karen reasoned, "maybe Wendy can use my eyes. Not all the time. She can borrow them."

"Sure," Sunee agreed, "and mine, too."

"Oh, girls, I love you for saying that, but you can't really lend her your eyes." Dorothy said. "It's like I can't lend you one of my legs. But you can help her. Wendy will be going to the hospital for a while, and when she comes home we hope that she'll be able to see out of her one eye. But, until then, you'll have to be her eyes.

"You'll have to lead her through the house. You'll have to show her where the toys are. You'll have to let her know about rules. It's not going to be easy, because she doesn't speak English. But you'll be able to make her understand. You sure will have a lot to do helping your little sister."

The two girls listened intently. Wendy wasn't going to be a threat to them. She was going to be their responsibility. They were obviously excited by the idea of helping another child.

The DeBolts brought Wendy home from the San Francisco airport on October 18, 1973, only three months after they had asked to adopt her. The poorly designed glass eye was obvious, and her live right eye was covered by a milky-white film. Both arms bore burn scars, and there were faint scars at the corners of her mouth. Dorothy wondered if they might be the result of deep malnutrition and dehydration sores.

The orphanage had reported that Wendy was introverted, reserved, and fearful of adults. When they got her home, Dorothy had each of them say his or her name as she guided Wendy's hands to their faces. Wendy occasionally broke into a tentative smile.

Dorothy and Bob then left her with the other children, who took turns in leading her around the rooms by her hand, talking to her, and moving her hand to door jambs and pieces of furniture. She followed meekly, neither resisting nor really participating.

Upstairs, Dorothy was changing into pants and a shirt when she heard laughter that was new to her. She looked at Bob and said, "It can't be who I think it is." They had reconciled themselves to an unhappy child and a rough period of adjustment.

They went downstairs. Dat and Trang had Wendy between them, holding her by the arms and swinging her up and down as they ran in circles around the spacious living room. The laughter came from Wendy. Once again, Dorothy realized how important the children were in making a new child become part of the family. Melanie, sprawled out on the sofa, asked her mother, "I thought you said she was gonna be sad."

"I thought she would be," Dorothy admitted.

And she was. On the next afternoon Sunee and Melanie were playing dolls with her when she suddenly turned from them and sat mute and buddhalike. She responded to nothing. Melanie handed her a doll, and she threw it away. She shrank from being touched. Then, after some twenty minutes, she suddenly changed again and reached for a doll. This "off" and "on" mood pattern confused the other girls.

Melanie asked her mother about it. Dorothy sat in the family room watching Wendy and trying to determine what prompted the pendulum swings in mood. "I don't know why Wendy acts like this," she confessed, "but don't push her. Let her be."

Later that afternoon Wendy cautiously began

climbing the staircase. Halfway up she sat down and began crying hard. Melanie put her arm around her and Wendy pushed her away. Dorothy sat beside her and talked softly, then touched her. Wendy shoved away her hand. "Oma!" she cried—the Korean word for "mother." "Oma!" she repeated.

Dorothy took her hand, "Oma," she said. "Oma here. I am Oma." She felt Wendy most likely was not calling for her actual mother: in Korean orphanages "Oma" was the woman supervising the child.

"No, no," Wendy cried. "Oma." After an hour she suddenly stopped, felt her way down the stairs and into the family room, and began playing with dolls.

On the following day Wendy repeated the performance, sitting on the stairs crying, raising her face and wailing toward the ceiling, saying over and over, "Oma." Dorothy picked her up and carried her screaming to her bedroom. Every ten minutes or so Dorothy returned to her and repeated in both English and Korean, "I love you," then left. Eventually Wendy fell asleep. When she awoke, she fumbled her way downstairs and across the front hall into the family room. Her ability to detect light and shadow enabled her to avoid obstacles and make her way from one room to another. She quickly learned to reach for a chair or table and work her way around it.

Bob was home during Wendy's third crying episode on the stairs. The weeping tore at his heart. "I can't stand it. She's got to stop that."

"Let her work it out," Dorothy advised. "If you want to, go over to her every once in a while and say something soothing."

But the crying went on for three hours, and

Dorothy couldn't stand it either. She finally went out to a picnic bench in the backyard and sat there until she felt calmer.

Wendy wasn't on the stairs when she went back inside. She heard no crying. Dorothy hurried upstairs and looked into Wendy's room. Thirteen-year-old Melanie was in a rocking chair with Wendy curled up in her arms. The older girl's face was streaked with tears. She looked up at her mother. Neither of them said a word.

To Dorothy, it seemed that Melanie had entered a conventionally self-centered, bratty stage, carping at and criticizing everything that went on in the house. Yet there she was feeling what Wendy was going through, giving the child love, taking care of her. Later, Dorothy told her, "You know, Melanie, sometimes I get teed off at you, but I think you're wonderful."

Melanie asked if she could phone Bob's daughter Doni in New Mexico and tell her about Wendy. Her parents agreed. They were both delighted with the relationship which had developed between their two thirteen-year-old daughters. Melanie, the quick and vivacious, and Doni, the sweet and open, had become comrades. Doni, who had at first felt threatened when her father married into this large family, was now one of the most enthusiastic advocates of more adoptions. "When's the next one coming?" she would push. "It's been over six months since we've had a new brother or sister!" If she was not present in Piedmont when a new child arrived, she insisted upon Melanie's giving her every detail of the new sibling's adjustments into the family.

Soon after Wendy's arrival Bob wondered about the glass eye. "We have no idea whether it should be removed each night, or left in, or washed, or boiled, or what," he told Dorothy. He called an opthalmologist, who instructed, "Leave it in as much as possible or that eye socket will start shrinking. Take it out every few days and wash it. I'll call in an antibiotic ointment prescription to your druggist. Put a little on the eye each time you clean it. Gently wash out the socket."

Bob hung up, then called the physician again. "How do you get the glass eye out?"

"Reach in with your finger. Not into the socket. Poke into the upper lid. You'll feel the eye. And just pop it out."

It worked easily enough, although Bob was tense and afraid of hurting Wendy.

Dorothy washed and coated the eye, then asked Bob, "How did the doctor say to put it back in?"

"I didn't ask him." The eye was an irregularly shaped oblong, far more flat than round. Neither of them could tell the bottom from the top. Bob looked at his wife's eyes. The glass eye had a light pink hue below one side of the pupil, as did Dorothy's eyes near her lower lid. So he knew which way was up, but he couldn't figure out whether the eye went in top or bottom first. He tried inserting the bottom of the eye first, but Wendy herself said, "No, no," took the eye from him, and inserted it topside first into the socket.

Another time, Dorothy had washed the eye and was carrying it back to Wendy, when she dropped it on the patterned rug. Dorothy was crawling around the room on all fours when Melanie came home from school.

"Mom, what in the heck are you doing?"

"I'm looking for Wendy's eye," Dorothy said, forlornly.

Melanie sighed—"This whole family is nuts!"—and joined the search.

Three ophthalmologists did several examinations of Wendy's live eye and the chief of the team reported, "We can't promise anything. There is a chance that the corneal transplant will be successful. But we really can't tell until we operate and get a good look at what's behind that film covering her eye. We may find cataracts or a problem involving the retina."

"What happened to her eyes?" Dorothy asked.

"I don't know. As an infant she may have developed an eye infection that was left untreated. A lack of proper nutrition probably compounded the results of the infection. The film developed and the eyes began to deteriorate."

"What happens next?"

"We wait for a cornea. You'll get twenty-four hours' notice. All we can do is hope that a right-sized cornea comes in soon. Time works against the eye."

Wendy remained withdrawn, weepy, and miserable. She also was hyperactive, sitting, standing, twisting her head, restlessly fumbling her way back and forth between rooms. Sunee and Karen were confused by her ability to avoid furniture and her inability to see a doll on the floor. Dorothy tried to explain light perception to them. They didn't understand, but accepted the fact that Wendy could do some things and not others with her eye.

The doctor called at 11:30 o'clock at night, twenty days after Wendy had joined the family. "I think we'll have a cornea within twenty-four hours," he reported. "Be prepared to bring Wendy to the hospital at eight A.M. Don't give her any food tomorrow morning. I'll call you as soon as I know something specific."

Dorothy was exhilarated. Bob said nothing. He had been struck by a thought that had not occurred to Dorothy. The cornea for Wendy was coming from a child about to die—coming thanks to that child's own parents. He couldn't wipe out the thought. It took him hours to fall asleep that night, and, when he did, he woke Dorothy with his tossing and teeth grinding.

At 7:00 A.M. the doctor called. "It looks as if we're going to get the cornea," he told Bob. "Bring Wendy in."

While Dorothy stayed with Wendy during her pre-surgical examination, Bob had a chance to ask his question: "Doctor, there's something on my mind. Where's the cornea coming from? Our daughter is gaining because other parents are losing. Can you tell me something about the source?"

"That information is not available to you and never will be," the doctor replied. "Stop thinking about that. Think in terms of hope for the kid getting the transplant. Look—there are just three things you can do with body tissue. You can bury it, or burn it, or use it. Why don't you just thank God that somebody has the good sense to want that cornea used? Sure, somebody is losing. It could have happened to the two of you or to my wife and me. But the couple who are making this contribution want to do it. They want something positive and good to come out of their loss, and that's why your daughter is getting the cornea."

It was a three-hour operation. Finally the doctor, still dressed in his green surgical gown, appeared. "I think she's going to see," he said. "When we got in there it was a hell of a lot worse than expected, but I believe it's going to work."

"When will you know?"

"After we remove her bandages. About a week."

Dorothy's hand shook when the call came. "We removed the bandages," she heard, "and the response is pretty good. She can see more. At this point everything is a kind of blur to her, but that should clear up if no complications set in."

Dorothy rushed to the hospital. Wendy was wearing a large, clear, plastic shield over her grossly swollen eye. Only a narrow slit separated the lids. Dorothy sat wordlessly on the edge of the bed. Wendy reached directly for her mother's cheeks. "Mommy," she said. Then she added, "Pretty."

Dorothy cradled and rocked her in her arms.

Each day brought improvement to the child's sight—and a radical change in her personality. She became spontaneously gay and outgoing. Everything entertained and enchanted her. The nurses, aides, and orderlies relished her joy and spent as much time as possible with her, teaching her English and identifying objects in picture books. Bob marveled at the transformation. "What a change in this child," he said to the doctor. "It's unbelievable."

"Don't you know what happened? Wendy sees. She thinks she died and went to Heaven. This is Heaven!

"I have to warn Dorothy and you about that eye," the doctor went on. "After Wendy leaves here, you must be very careful about protecting it. Any disturbance or blow to it can cause the loss of the cornea. And we can't go back and do it again. I'll tell you this now and I'll keep repeating it. The eye will have to be protected for a considerable time and drops must be administered to it religiously. We've lost corneas in children because parents have become sloppy about the drops or because a kid bumped his unprotected eye four months after the operation. Just remember that if she loses the cornea, the eye will be nothing more than a useless piece of pulp. The shield stays on night and day. After nine or ten months Wendy can switch to glasses during the day."

At home Wendy peered closely at each child, put her hands to their cheeks, said their names, and laughed aloud. She went to a window and stared at the shrubbery and trees. She touched and studied the dolls. She examined all the tables and chairs that she had known only by touch. Everything delighted her: cornflakes poured from the box; photographs on the wall; Dorothy's fingers moving across the keys of the piano; the autumn leaves drifting to earth. Sometimes in her exuberance she ran in circles in the front hall like a playful puppy. Where she had been remote before the operation, she now seemed to crave affection. She would touch and gently hold Dorothy's hand. She clutched Bob's legs in greeting when he returned from his office. A tiny sliver of tissue and surgical skill, in opening the world for her, had opened Wendy herself.

Every few days Bob tested her: "What's this?" She reached out and grabbed the pencil. Then he stood Trang about ten feet from her and asked, "Wendy, who's this? Tich?"

"No."

"Melanie?"

"No."

"Trang?"

"Yes."

About a month after her return from the hospital she and Bob were in the backyard. Wendy suddenly pointed to the sky and talked in rapid pidgin English and Korean. She was directing Bob's attention to a thread-thin contrail made by an aircraft so high that it was invisible. There was also dramatic vision improvement at short range. When a few grains of rice fell from her plate at the table one night Wendy meticulously picked up each one.

Wendy's disposition was like her face: delightfully happy and open. There was an honesty to that wide face and broad features; her beauty lay in her liveliness and humor. Wendy so enjoyed life, her family and the very existence of everything around her, that she could not contain herself. She jumped about, laughing, talking, and continually interrupting others. She wasn't being rude or self-centered; she simply was bursting with feelings and thoughts. When Sunee reminded her, "Wendy, we've told you over and over not to interrupt someone who's talking," Wendy contritely closed her lips and hung her head, but within a few seconds she again interrupted. She was incorrigible. Months later, on the evening of Wendy's first summer kindergarten, when Bob asked her about the experience, she said she'd had a good day. "Did the teacher talk to you?" "Yes." "What did she say?" " 'Sit down and be quiet.' " And one day at breakfast when she was jabbering away and going to be late, Bob finally said, "If you don't stop talking I'm going to take your plate away from you."

Wendy looked at him, then at her bowl, still filled with her favorite cereal, then back at Bob. She considered carefully. Then she said, "Good-bye, breakfast."

Wendy also was inordinately clumsy, some of it due to her having only one eye. She had to learn to perceive depth and gauge distance. When it was her turn to set the table she pulled the utensil drawer completely out of the cabinet—and laughed as knives, forks, and spoons clattered around her feet. Dorothy once asked her to empty a kitchen garbage pail into the large container along the driveway. Wendy ran to do the chore. Outside, she raised the pail high and turned it upside down, backward, dumping eggshells, coffee grounds, cantaloupe rinds, empty milk cartons, and cans over her own head. Later, she fell off the toilet seat.

Once when Trang put the dog's food bowl on the kitchen floor, Bob said, "Don't leave that bowl there. If Wendy comes through she's bound to step in it."

"I'll tell her about it," Trang said, and called to Wendy, who was in the family room. She darted into the kitchen and stepped into the bowl before Trang could utter a word.

Nobody kept count of the number of times she inadvertently knocked over her milk while eating. In the beginning, just after her corneal transplant when her vision was minimal, she'd had her meals in the old family high chair so that the few things she had to cope with on its tray might be simpler, separated from the busy family table. But this didn't help much—more often than not the milk wound up on the floor—so Wendy took her place at the table with the rest. After a few full cups streamed across the tabletop, Dorothy or Bob began pouring her an inch of milk at a time. She still knocked it over. Then began nightly experiments at placing the cup in a spot where she couldn't hit it with her hands, elbows, or utensils. Wendy tried. She carefully picked up the cup, drank some milk, then placed the cup on the rim of the dinner plate where it toppled over. She usually sat on Bob's left, and he became quite agile at jumping out of his chair to avoid receiving the milk in his lap.

Wendy gradually learned where to put the milk so it wouldn't spill. One night Dorothy decided it was time to compliment her. "Wendy, you're doing a good job of not spilling your milk. We're so proud of you." Wendy thanked her mother, picked up her cup, took a swallow, then took the cup away from her mouth without turning it up again. The rest of the milk landed in her lap.

Bob took the three little girls to get ice cream cones one afternoon and had settled them in the back end of the station wagon—on the bare metal—to eat them. He had just finished warning them that he didn't want any spilled ice cream, when Wendy turned enthusiastically to agree with him and thereby jammed her cone into Karen's face. Bob was prepared with a stack of napkins; he was wiping Karen down when he heard Sunee say, "Oh, Wendy." He looked up to see Wendy sitting cross-legged, her arms on the floor of the wagon, an empty cone in her hand, looking at the mound of ice cream melting between her legs.

The only aspect of Wendy's clumsiness that seriously worried the DeBolts was the possibility of damage to her eye. During her first few weeks of vision she frequently walked into door jambs and closet doors. Once she ran into a jamb so hard that the impact split the shield. But somehow the eye continued to escape injury.

Wendy refused to answer questions about her earlier life. She rapidly dropped the use of Korean words. But occasionally she volunteered a piece of information. One night, Dorothy was putting the child to bed while

Sunee and Karen were picking up the toys in the family room. As she watched Wendy wriggle into a nightgown she impulsively said, "Wendy, I love you so much. I'm so glad you're my little girl."

Wendy, her tongue between her teeth, considered that comment for a moment, then said, "My mommy didn't like me."

Dorothy was startled. "Everybody likes you, Wendy."

"My mommy didn't."

"Maybe she was sick and worried and just acted as if she didn't like you."

"She just didn't like me." There was no bitterness or resentment in her tone. She was making a statement of fact.

"Well, you've got a mommy now who loves you."

"Yep."

The following September, in 1974, Bob escorted Wendy to the Wildwood Elementary School to introduce her and himself to the first-grade teacher. He was outlining Wendy's history for the teacher's information—interspersing his remarks with, "Wendy, don't play with those papers. . . . Put down that pen. . . . Don't wander off, stay here. . . . Why don't you just sit down for a few minutes?"—when the woman noticed a big scar on Wendy's arm and remarked about it.

Wendy heard it and offhandedly said, "They threw me in the fire."

The teacher looked in consternation at the child. Bob was taken aback. He wished for a clever way to change the subject. He and Dorothy had decided not to ask Wendy about the scars for fear of disturbing her needlessly. This was her first voluntary reference to them.

"My mommy didn't love me," Wendy continued.

Bob said, "Well, now your mommy loves you very much. Nothing like that can ever happen now."

Wendy nodded. Very seriously she said, "No, now everything is all right."

Some time later a visitor from Japan noticed the scars and asked if Wendy came from Korea. The scars were familiar to him—he had seen them in the remote villages there. When a child had a serious, persistent affliction, she was considered to be possessed by the devil, which could be exorcised by a fire ritual. Sticks, inserted at specific points in the body, were lighted and allowed to burn down into the flesh.

A few days after the school incident Bob playfully called Wendy by her Korean name. "Kim Kwan Ok," he began, "do you—"

"Don't say that!" Wendy was suddenly very agitated. She frowned and twisted her hands. "Don't say that! That not my name. I Wendy. I Wendy."

Bob felt guilt-stricken. He had not seen the child so distraught since her operation. "You're right, you're right," he assured her. "You're Wendy. You're our little girl."

But for the rest of the day Wendy was distracted. Early that evening Dorothy was alone in her bedroom, and Wendy hesitantly entered. Her lips were pursed. "Mommy, when you send me to Korea?"

Dorothy was surprised. "What do you mean?"

"When I have to go back?"

Dorothy thought for a moment. Bob had told her of the incident. The child Wendy belonged to this family in Piedmont, but the child Kim Kwan Ok belonged in Korea.

"Honey, you live here now. You're not going back to Korea. Not ever. This is your home."

A look of relief crossed Wendy's face. "That's good," she said, "I don't want leave sisters." Then she quietly left the room and hurried down the stairs to join Sunee and Karen.

Dorothy came down the driveway.

"Mommy! I have present for you!"

"Oh, nice, Wendy. What beautiful daisies! Twe, it's time to go to the doctor."

Twe rose from the swing and began walking slowly across the lawn. Meanwhile Dorothy picked up the basketball, dribbled it across the concrete patio, and shot a couple of baskets into the net mounted on a post on the other side. At fifty-two she was lithe and smooth-muscled and moved the basketball easily and accurately. At that moment Trang, back from his afternoon paper route, hurried down the driveway and Dorothy tossed the ball to him. Then she took Twe's hand.

"Kids," she said, "you all have things to do this afternoon and you'd better go in and get started. I don't know how long we'll be gone, but Dad's in the house—he's working in the bedroom."

Trang took the handles of Lee's wheelchair, got a good running start on the flat surface, and ran the chair up the steep driveway to the side steps. Then he ran back and did the same with J.R., who was patiently waiting. Dorothy had put the cup of daisies into his lap, and he was balancing it carefully. The other children straggled along behind, and Dorothy and Twe went up to the car.

Phong ran to the basement, filled two wicker baskets with clothes from the dryer, and made two trips to the family room, where he put the baskets on the dining-room table. Lee was waiting for them. Wendy hopped over and joined Lee in folding and sorting the laundry. Sunee went to the living-room piano to practice her lessons. Karen went into the book-lined library and settled herself at the marimba. She swung the mallets with an intensity that was almost ferocious.

J.R. rolled his chair into the front hall, parked near a side table, and slid down from the chair. He groped under the table and found the 5-pound barbell. Slowly and lackadaisically he raised and lowered the weight. He recognized Bob's fast steps down the staircase and said, "Hi, Dad."

"Hi, J.R." Bob watched for several seconds, then said, "J.R., what are you doing?"

"I'm exercising."

"Is it hard?"

"Not very."

"It's got to be hard or it isn't exercise." Bob's tone was edged with anger. "Do it fast. Do it until that barbell feels as if it weighs a ton—then keep on doing it. You've got to build up those muscles. It'll take strain and sweat. All your brothers and sisters did it, and so can you. Not one of them could climb the nineteen steps in that staircase when they arrived. Now they all can without any trouble. That's your goal, J.R. Those steps are this family's Mount Everest. But you won't be able to conquer it if your mother and I have to keep reminding you to exercise properly. What do you think about when you lift that weight?"

"Nothing."

"Think about standing up on crutches and braces.

Think about walking. Think about climbing those steps. Remember, you're going to walk for your own sake. You have to want to do it because it's going to make your life better. Not Mom's. Not mine. Yours. Do you want to sit like a damn lump in that chair for the rest of your life?"

"No." J.R.'s face was expressionless.

"We can't get you out of that chair, J.R. We can't wish you out of it. And you can't daydream your way out of it. Only determination and work on your part will do it. Understand?"

"Yes, Dad."

His voice softening, Bob said, "I'm talking to you like this, J.R., because we care about you. You're our son. We love you." He paused. "Now pick up that weight, and when I come back I want to see sweat."

Bob strode into the kitchen, his face grim. Tich and Anh had overheard him. Anh said, "J.R. need pushin', huh, Bob?"

"And how. I chew him out and I get no reaction from him. I'd like to see him get sore, angry. I'd like him to say to himself, 'I'll show that so-and-so that I can climb those stairs. If the others can do it, I can do it. And when I do it, I'm going to take that damn barbell and throw it at him.' "

Tich said, "Maybe it take a little time. J.R. not here very long."

"I know. But it'll be a good thing when he isn't afraid to show anger and say something that other people won't like."

Two hours later the telephone rang. Tich and Anh had brought in some zucchini from the garden, and Bob was washing it to cook for dinner. He dried his hands and picked up the phone. He listened for almost a minute, then said, "That's terrific, Dorothy . . . great . . . we'll hold dinner until you get here."

He hung up and told Tich and Anh, "That was Mom. The doctor thinks there's a good chance that a corneal transplant will work on Twe's one eye. The other eye, the one that's sunken, is gone, hopeless. But if she gets to see, what a thing that'll be! Can you imagine!"

Tich said, "Yeah. I remember Wendy. She became new kid when she got transplant."

Anh said, "Bet I know what Mom doing."

Bob laughed. "What?"

"Crying."

"You're right."

"Mom always cry when she's happy. Something I never get used to. A person crying 'cause she's happy."

nine

About three months after Wendy joined the family an article about the DeBolts appeared in *The New York Times* of January 22, 1974. It included:

> The DeBolts' concern over what happens—or rather, doesn't happen—to handicapped homeless children both here and abroad has become so serious that this fall they created a non-profit foundation called Aid to the Adoption of Special Kids (P.O. Box 11212, Oakland, California 94611). It is designed specifically to recruit families to adopt children who are physically or mentally handicapped, of minority descent or more than nine years old.

The feature attracted a flurry of letters to P.O. Box 11212. Some praised the DeBolts. Most writers wanted to know more about the kinds of children that were available for adoption. But there was one letter from a New York City nurse, who wrote:

> Recently we had a patient, John, aged nine years, who is a paraplegic as a result of congenital spina bifida. In addition John has been blind since age five. I do not have great details of John's past experiences, but I

would like to tell you about him as he is now. He is desperately in need of a home, preferably adoptive but certainly long-term foster care would be a great help.

John came to our hospital in November, 1973, ostensibly to get treatment for a urinary tract infection. In reality, the foster mother who had been caring for him had a psychotic breakdown and the agency responsible for John was forced to provide emergency placement for this child and for two other seriously handicapped children who were also in the same home. John stayed with us until two weeks ago (we are not a long-term health facility) at which time he was transferred to Blythedale Hospital, a convalescent and rehabilitation hospital in Valhalla, New York.

John is a bright child intellectually. He did well in school (we have a public school teacher working with our hospitalized children) and reads and writes Braille. He showed great warmth with the nurses. John can take care of himself quite well. He needs assistance to apply leg braces which might allow him to walk with the help of Canadian crutches.

If no home can be found for this child within the next six months, he will be placed in an institution set up for crippled children.

Dorothy discovered from her own family's pediatrician that spina bifida was a defect in the spinal cord and spinal column. It meant that John was helpless from the waist down and had no bladder or bowel control. The defect often caused spinal fluid to collect in the head, which possibly accounted for John's blindness.

In further correspondence with the nurse, Dorothy learned that John's handicaps were indeed formidable— he had already had several operations to deal with spinal fluid—but that he had spirit and intelligence. He had mastered braille, was getting help with his braces, and now had a wheelchair with a one-wheel drive so he could use a pointer cane with his free hand. Adoption inquiries should be addressed to Spence-Chapin—the agency that had brought Karen to the DeBolts.

Dorothy could find no one in the AASK files who wanted to take John. There were families willing to adopt a spina bifida child, but not one that was blind as well; such a combination of handicaps seemed too overwhelming.

Finally she said to Bob one night over dinner, "There's no better home than ours for John. We've had experience with all his problems. I think we should adopt him, Bob." Bob agreed.

It was a Friday night in June. On the following Monday she telephoned the Spence-Chapin director, Jane Edwards, and asked, "Have you heard from anyone about wanting John?"

"No, not a call or a letter."

"Well, you've got the call now. We want him."

"What?"

"Bob and I want to adopt John. We've talked it over and it's the right thing to do."

Mrs. Edwards broke into tears. "Dorothy," she said, "today happens to be John's birthday."

Plans for picking up John in the East were set for some months ahead, in November. In the meanwhile the family sent him tape recorded greetings telling him about themselves and their eagerness to have him. Dorothy wrote to the hospital, "December will be devoted to John. *He* will be our Christmas!" and she sent John a calendar so he could pull off a page every day and know the time until his adoption was growing shorter and shorter.

During the early part of the summer two major events happened in the family: Bob decided to give up his job as president of the engineering firm so that he could give more time to AASK: he would work, on a more flexible schedule, as an engineering consultant. (It would mean a definite loss of income, but both Dorothy and Bob felt the job of running AASK was more important than any salaried job.) Hardly had Bob cleared his desk at the office when Dorothy received a call from a friend who had adopted two handicapped Korean boys originally brought to her attention by the DeBolts. Her call was about an eight-year-old Vietnamese boy named Phong.

Phong had been sent to this country by an uncle after his parents had been killed in a rocket explosion. He had lived for a while with each of three aunts, but the aunts were single, had to work, and could not afford a housekeeper for the boy. They had appealed to the Children's Home Society for help, and Phong was placed in a foster home—but not for long. Financial contributions from the aunts for the child's support were irregular and insufficient, and the foster family could not afford to keep him. Since the child was a Vietnamese citizen, he was not eligible for state aid. He had been shunted from one foster home to another, a situation that was bound to take its toll on him. Phong was a beautiful, gentle, healthy child, a natural for adoption, but the uncle had refused to permit it.

The phone call was to ask Dorothy if she knew of any Vietnamese who might contact the uncle with a further appeal for adoption release. A young Vietnamese priest and the Vietnamese consul general in San

Francisco were both put in touch with the uncle, but their efforts failed. The consul then asked if the DeBolts would become Phong's temporary guardians, and Dorothy and Bob said they would. They moved Phong in with fourteen-year-old Trang in the basement bedroom, and Trang took on the role of mentor to the younger boy. Phong, who was bright and alert, made the adjustment to his new home with predictable smoothness. He enjoyed his share of the family chores. He never forgot to fill the school lunch bags with sandwiches and fruit for the three girls and himself, and each Saturday he swept the driveway. The first time he took a turn at saying grace at the dinner table, he said: "Thank you for letting me play in the yard with Karen and Sunee and Wendy. Thank you for letting me sweep the driveway. Thank you for everything. Thank you for everybody."

In September 1974, Bob enrolled eight-year-old Sunee in the second grade at the Wildwood Elementary School. The DeBolts felt she no longer needed a school for the handicapped, that she could function on a day-to-day basis with the able-bodied. After Sunee returned from her first day, Dorothy asked her how it went and she apathetically answered, "All right, I guess. One boy pointed to me and called me a 'nut.' "

"Don't be upset by it," Dorothy said. "Feel sorry for him. He hasn't been taught to be nice to people."

A few weeks later the family had a turkey dinner, and Bob offered the wishbone to two teams: Sunee and Phong on one, Wendy and Karen on the other. Afterward, Sunee, one of the winners, asked Bob, "Do wishes come true?"

"Some do. But mostly it's the fun. It's fun to make wishes even if they don't come true."

"Well, I guess my wish probably won't come true."

"What was your wish?"

"Just a silly wish. But it's a secret."

"All right."

"But I'll tell you if you won't tell anyone else."

"Okay, I promise."

"I wish I could walk like the other kids at school."

Bob took a measured breath. "Well, that's a pretty rough wish to have come true. You know, I'll bet some of those kids wish they could do things that you can do. Like play the piano. And read books as if you were a fourth grader instead of a second grader."

"Yes," Sunee said brightly. "I am pretty good at those things."

But school remained a disturbing experience. "Those kids at school!" she told Dorothy. "When you have a handicap they look at you and look at you and look at you." She made a face, mimicking an open stare of curiosity.

"Does it still bother you, honey?"

"Sometimes it does."

"Well, try to understand. Those kids don't know about handicaps. They have no handicapped children in their homes. They don't know how much you can do. Sunee, some of those kids may laugh at you and make fun of your handicap. That can happen. Just be friendly and smile. Once they get to know you and know what you can do, they'll stop. Sunee, let them put on braces and crutches and try to do what you do. They'd fall flat on their faces. You're a pretty special person in that school. You're the only one that's physically handicapped."

Sunee said, "Yes." She said it proudly.

Dorothy kept stressing the advantages of being different from other children until one conversation showed her that she had mishandled the problem. "You have a right to be proud of yourself, Sunee," she said, "You've accomplished so much. Tell me, what can you do that other children can't do?"

"Wear braces."

Dorothy was startled. "That's just a small part of you. What else?"

"I had polio."

"No, no, sweetheart. That *happened* to you. What are the really special things you can do?"

"I can put both my legs around my neck."

Dorothy changed tack. "Sunee, everybody is different from everybody else. Everybody has some kind of defect. Some boys and girls wear glasses. Their eyes aren't as good as yours. Some don't do as well in school as you because their brains aren't as good as yours. See what I mean? So your legs aren't as good as theirs. What can't you do that they can do? You can't run from one place to another. All right. It takes you a little longer. You can't climb a tree. Big deal."

"That's right," Sunee said eagerly, suddenly getting the point. "That's right."

By her second term she stopped referring to her handicap. The pupils in school apparently lost interest in her crutches and braces. They gave her no special attention. Her classwork, which had been sloppy or uncompleted, sharply improved. She looked forward to school each morning.

The week of Dorothy's and Bob's departure to pick up John was hectic. It was just before Thanksgiving, and when they returned with him there would be a big holiday reunion that had been planned for months.

They expected every one of the children except Kim for Thanksgiving dinner. Dorothy had been cooking for days before she and Bob left for New York, and most of the feast was ready in the freezer.

A few evenings before they left, they heard Mimi, who was to be in charge of the household during their absence, talking on the second-floor hall telephone. She said, "No, I haven't worked it out yet, Noël. Not completely. I'll get to it after I hang up." Noël was in Phoenix at Arizona State University.

Then Mimi knocked on their bedroom door and asked, "Can I talk to you about something?"

"Sure," said Bob.

"I've been thinking about this Thanksgiving," Mimi opened, "and how great it will be for all of us to be together—and with our new brother John being here and being a part of our Thanksgiving for the first time. I've been talking with the other children, Mom and Dad, and we are all of the same mind. We'd like Kim to be here at Thanksgiving."

"Well, I'm not sure that—" Dorothy began.

Mimi interrupted her. "I've talked to Kim about it. It was my idea. He said he wanted to be a part of the family again, but he didn't know how to do it and whether or not you wanted him back."

"He has always known that the door is open to him," Dorothy answered. "He's known that he's been welcome to dinner. But at this time . . . We're so busy. We're dealing with a new child. Why does he pick now?"

"Mom, Kim wasn't ready before," Mimi pleaded. "Now he is. He wants to come back. We're a family, and we want the family—the whole family—to be together this Thanksgiving. All the kids want Kim to be here. We want your approval."

"Let Bob and me talk it over for a few minutes," Dorothy said. Mimi left them alone and Dorothy thought for a moment. Was *she* ready? Then she said to Bob, "Resentment doesn't achieve a lot, does it?" She went to tell Mimi that she'd like Kim to come.

Several days later Bob braked the car to a stop in front of the house. Everyone except Kim had arrived home for the holiday, and there were fourteen who came one by one out the door to the porch. "This is it!" said Bob. "Hey, there's a big sign posted saying 'WEL- COME TO THE FAMILY, JOHN.' They don't know your new name yet, do they?" John had decided to add "Robert" as his middle name, after his new father, and they had begun calling him "J.R."

All the children gathered around this boy with the soft brown hair and strangely clear blind eyes, and then Dorothy and Bob hugged them all amid shouts and laughter. It had been almost a year since they'd seen Steffi, who at twenty-four was working as an instructor in an Outward Bound program in Texas, and Mike, twenty-six, and Marty, twenty, who'd flown home from Hawaii. Mike was now working toward his commercial pilot's license while finishing his year of half-time service at the school for the handicapped. Marty was looking forward to a career in the nursery business.

It was Trang who wheeled J.R. into the family room. Sunee, Karen, Phong, and Wendy followed them. Karen swung on her crutches to a big steamer trunk and said, "John—I mean J.R.—come on over here. I want to show you our dolls and our books and our games."

171

J.R. said, "Someone will have to push me over. I can't see."

"That's right," Karen said. "Mommy and Daddy told us you were blind. You mean you can't see nothing? At all?"

"No."

"Wendy was once blind, weren't you, Wendy?"

"That's right," Wendy chirped. "But I can hardly remember. Mommy and Daddy took me to the hospital where they gave me a new eye. The other eye is just a thing. It comes out."

Trang corrected her. "It's not a new eye, Wendy. It's a corneal transplant."

"It's a new eye," Wendy insisted.

Karen said, "J.R., maybe you can go to the hospital for a new eye."

J.R. said nothing.

During supper Anh sat next to J.R. at a low square table in the kitchen. J.R. touched his fried chicken with his fork. Then he put the fork down.

Anh said, "You not hungry?"

"I can't cut the chicken."

"Why not? You got two good hands."

"The food was always cut up for me."

"J.R., you gotta get with it here. We start right now. My God, Karen has two hooks for hands and she can do it." He put a knife and fork in J.R.'s hands, then guided them through the cutting. "Take a little time, J.R., but you'll get it. Around here, nobody do things like that for nobody else. You better learn pretty fast, else you get very skinny from not eating."

When J.R. finished eating Anh looked at his plate and said, "You left your squash."

"I don't like squash."

172

"A lot of thing you don't like?"

"Well, some."

"J.R., you gotta learn about family. Everybody here gotta right not eat one food. Melanie can't stand cauliflower. I think string beans for the birds, Okay. But outside that one thing, you gotta eat everything. This is big family, and food expensive. We don't throw away. What you don't eat at dinner get put in refrigerator, and you get for breakfast. You wanna skip breakfast, then you get for lunch. Not long before you learn eat food on your plate."

After dinner Dorothy played some of the children's old favorites on the piano and everybody sang. At about nine o'clock she suddenly began to feel queasy and lightheaded, and Bob too felt sick. Both had temperatures, and they decided to go to bed. J.R. had already gone into the first-floor bedroom, and Bob asked Anh, who was his appointed help and mentor, to take charge of him.

J.R. had put his clothes away in drawers and was trying to get from the wheelchair onto the bed. He didn't have the necessary strength in his arms to make it, and Anh gave him a hand.

"J.R., this no good," Anh said. "We got a lot of work ahead. Here, feel my arms and shoulders. Now feel yours. Big difference, huh? That come from lifting weights and doing pushups. You gonna do that, J.R. You really gonna sweat. Your arms gotta lift your whole weight. Can't get too fat. You a little heavy. After you do a lot of sweatin', you gonna get outta wheelchair and walk on crutches."

Anh paused. Then he said, "J.R., everything gonna be all right. I same as you when I came here. Pretty scared. Everything strange. You get over it. You got a mom and dad and brothers and sisters. You got a family. You go to sleep now. I won't be far away."

Still J.R. looked tentative, unsettled. Anh said, "Bag empty?"

"No. It's different from yours, though."

Anh knew this. J.R.'s was an ileal conduit, a urine bag affixed to a nickel-sized opening in his abdomen. Bob had told him about it before J.R. ever arrived. "Okay. You need help, right?"

"Mom and Dad forgot."

"They not forget. They know I know about that kind." When Anh had arrived in the states, he'd been in crisis three times from bladder infections and had had an ileal conduit himself. "Okay. We fix you up, J.R."

Dorothy and Bob awoke about eight o'clock on Thanksgiving morning feeling much better. They found Mimi, Melanie, and Doni in the kitchen organizing things for breakfast. Mimi poured them each a cup of coffee, and Dorothy had just sat down with hers when she remembered a basket of laundry she'd meant to bring down for washing. She went upstairs to get it, and when she came down again she ran almost bodily into Kim, who had just come in through the side door.

She dropped the basket on a bench. "Well, for crying out loud!" she exclaimed, and threw open her arms. "It's great to have you here, Kim."

"It's great to be here, Mom."

His arms around her felt stronger than she had remembered, and she realized that Kim had grown from an adolescent to a young man. They separated and looked at each other. Dorothy saw that his eyes were wet. "I'm nowhere near tears," she thought, surprised. "This isn't real."

Next Dat arrived, enthusiastic and ebullient. He had moved out of the house the previous January after his graduation from high school and was living with his older brothers in San Francisco, where he went to a junior college.

He threw his arms around Dorothy. This was the same boy who had always been reluctant to show physical affection. She hugged him back.

The telephone never stopped ringing. Friends of the children began dropping in. The three breakfast cooks were busy preparing eggs Florentine and baking cinnamon rolls.

Anh wheeled J.R. into the family room, where about twenty-five people were laughing, talking, and greeting each other. Dorothy met him with a kiss, noticing that J.R. was smiling and relaxed. Marty was smiling too. He had an easy assurance that was new to Dorothy. He seemed comfortable with himself. He had received his high-school diploma and was working as a maintenance worker on a coffee plantation and as a landscape gardener for a hotel. He loved to work with the soil. He was planning to enter a junior college to study forestry and horticulture. She felt good about him now. Somewhere in his development after he had left home he had lost his feeling of inferiority. He liked himself—had faced himself and discovered that he could respect what he saw. And he had retained his sweetness and concern for others.

As the day went on, Kim floated easily into the family stream of talk and activity. All the older children had been away; now they were home and he was one of them. It was as though his going away those years ago had been just as untraumatic and inevitable as theirs.

When the family gathered around the buffet spread

out in the living room that evening—the two hams, two turkeys, beans and breads and salads—Bob asked Dorothy if she'd like to say grace. She looked around her and began, "Thank you, God, for . . ." and couldn't go on.

After dinner there was music, piano, guitars, voices filling the room. During a pause Karen asked, "Can Sunee, Wendy, and me put on a show?"

"Sure! Show time!" Dorothy said, pounding the piano.

"Play boogie-woogie, Mom," Karen said and unstrapped her plastic arms and legs. Sunee took off her braces too, and Wendy joined in the fun. Unencumbered by heavy prostheses, Karen and Sunee exuberantly danced around, stopping, rolling, swinging their bodies to the rhythm of the music. Karen did headstands, multiple somersaults, and darted and squirmed nimbly back and forth across the floor.

J.R., in his wheelchair next to Dorothy, said, "Mom, can I dance in the next show?"

"Of course. You can dance anytime you want to."

His eyes were shining. "I have to dance right now. I have to. Is that all right?"

"Go right ahead, honey."

He lifted himself off the wheelchair seat by straightening his arms, then shook his bottom to the beat of the music, the rhythmic applause of the older children and the shouts of "Attaboy, J.R.!" "Go, J.R., go!" When he finished, panting and flushed, Dorothy saw a look of unalloyed joy on his face.

The following morning Dorothy felt miserable. She again had a fever. Bob told her to stay in bed; he'd take care of things downstairs. He found that J.R. had had diarrhea during the night, and his urine bag had leaked. Everything—sheets, pajamas, blankets—was a mess. Anh awoke to Bob's cry of "Oh, no!" and they spent an hour running the bedclothes through washing machines, scrubbing and disinfecting the floor around the bed, and getting J.R. bathed.

On J.R.'s third night with the family Dorothy was feeling much better, and she joined the family downstairs after dinner. Sunee said, "Dad, can we wrestle with you?"

"Sure," Bob said.

"Would you call Phong? With him we can beat you."

"Oh, you think so?" Bob said, grinning. "Well, you're in for a surprise."

"Can I do it too?" J.R. asked eagerly. "I'm going to try to get out of the wheelchair and down to the floor by myself. I've never done that." He pushed himself forward, slid down the front of the chair, and began to drag himself across the floor toward the others. Bob had called Phong on the house intercom and was now sprawled passively on his back on the rug, waiting for the kids to pounce. At first J.R. wanted to see more than to play, and the boy felt Bob's nose and chin. He crawled to Dorothy, and she leaned down from her chair while he felt her hair and face and arms. He ran a hand around Karen's arm stumps and hips. "Will Karen grow legs?"

"No," Dorothy said. "Karen was born without legs and she will have to get along with artificial legs and crutches."

His hand went over Wendy's face. He recognized

her giggle, and said, "I didn't know you wore glasses, Wendy." Then he touched Sunee's fine, soft hair and lifeless legs.

Phong ran into the room, and he and the other three children burst into action. All five, including J.R., tried to pin down Bob's four limbs and tickle him into submission. He tried to capture three of them in a scissor lock with his legs while he held the other two squirming in his arms. The children scrambled and slipped from his holds with shouts, yelps, and laughter—all except J.R., who decided to rest in the crook of Bob's arm for a while. Meanwhile hands darted at Bob, tickling his belly and ribs. After several minutes of rough play—everyone was perspiring a little—Bob was pinned to the floor while the children knuckled his midriff. Laughing, he cried, "Okay, okay—I give up. You win."

He arose, pushing back his hair with a hand. Karen and Sunee clutched his legs and he bent down and kissed them goodnight. Then he kissed Wendy and Phong. He lifted J.R. into his wheelchair and pushed him into the kitchen toward the bedroom on the other side. "I'll help you get ready for bed."

"I want to try to do it myself. I think I can."

Using his probe, J.R. slowly and cautiously wheeled himself through the kitchen's length between cooking island and the sink counters, across a small hallway, then made a left turn into the bathroom. With a smile on his face, Bob watched him go.

After the long weekend there was the inevitable exit of the visiting members of the family, and even Mimi left, to go with Mike and Marty to Hawaii so she could see what life was like there. J.R. seemed to settle into the family pattern fairly well, but he spent much of his time in silence, his head bent slightly sideways, his sightless eyes immobile, his thoughts obviously far away.

About a week before Christmas when Bob was having a goodnight chat with him, J.R. said, "Dad, there's something I've been thinking about. When did Mom and you decide to adopt me?"

"During the summer before we brought you home."

"But you didn't bring me home until just before Thanksgiving. Remember? So you must have made up your mind at that time."

"No, J.R., we decided long before that. Didn't the social workers tell you? Don't you remember the tape we sent you about how eager we were to adopt you? When we came to New York it was just to sign the papers and go through the formalities and pick you up."

"Well, that isn't what they told me at the hospital. They said you'd make up your mind when you were visiting me."

"That's not so, J.R."

The boy sighed. "I was scared. They said that when you got to the hospital you might decide not to adopt me."

Bob concealed his anger at hearing this. "I'm sorry you were put through that worry. But that's over. You're home. Can you believe that?"

"Yes."

In their bedroom Bob repeated the conversation to Dorothy. "There was no need to make the kid suffer for months," he told her, tossing his shirt into the bathroom hamper and slamming the lid. "Maybe those hospital people wanted to prepare him for the worst, but nothing would have softened J.R.'s disappointment if he had been rejected. Why do they have to be so negative? Why do they have to create fear? They could just as easily have told him, 'Hey, things look pretty good. This family really seems to want you.'"

Dorothy said soothingly, "It's over. We couldn't do anything about a situation that we knew nothing about. And the fact that J.R. opened up about it must mean that he's feeling secure here."

But J.R. wasn't sure of his status. On the following night, when Bob said goodnight to him, he was silent. Bob put a hand to his cheek and asked, "Are you okay, J.R.?"

"Can I ask a question?"

"Sure. What's on your mind?"

The boy fidgeted uneasily with some braille cards. "Have there been any kids who came into this family"—he was stuttering now—"and didn't stay here?"

Bob understood what he really wanted to ask. "Oh, sure. We've had kids from other countries who've stayed with us for a while until they got their affairs straightened out and found a permanent place. They understood that they were only visiting. But, J.R., no adopted child has ever had to leave. You have to realize, old buddy, that when we adopted you, you became our son forever and ever. And you took us for your father and mother forever and ever."

J.R. considered the statement for a few moments, took a deep breath, and said, "That's good."

Christmas came, and another family reunion, except for the three in Hawaii. Kim came again, walking quietly into the kitchen where Dorothy was working at a counter and tapping her on the shoulder. When she turned, he said, "I love you, Mom." She put her arms around him. "I love you too, Kim," she said.

During the day they all exchanged presents, and they recorded their feelings on a tape—a Christmas tradition since Bob and Dorothy's marriage. Kim's part said, "I haven't shared Christmas with the family for a while. It's something I needed and wanted to do, and the feeling I have is hard to express. . . . A family is where you're always comfortable. I haven't felt family love for a long time and it's really special to share in it again."

Doni, Bob's fourteen-year-old daughter, who until the age of ten had been an only child, wrote a poem as a gift to the family:

How can a person say, "I love you,"
When no words can explain how you feel
When you love in so many different ways
That your head begins to reel?
I guess what I'm really trying to say is that
I love you all more than you'll ever, ever know.
You've all taught me how to look at a handicapped person
And not see his or her braces or wheelchair,
But to see deep inside him and see his soul.
All of you have made me a better and happier person.
I used to think I had my eyes open,
But all I could see was me.
Now, all of you have set me free.

While Bob and Dorothy were in J.R.'s room that night the boy suddenly threw his arms around Dorothy and began to cry. "What is it?" Dorothy said. "Tell us. Does something hurt?"

Between sobs, words spilled out of him: "I don't

want to go to sleep . . . there's love here . . . I've never been part of anything like this . . . I don't want to go to sleep . . . I've been in places where there was so much fighting . . . not love, like here . . . I don't want to go to sleep . . . afraid . . . I'm afraid I'll wake up and find it isn't true . . . that it's a dream."

"It's true, J.R.," Dorothy assured him. "All true. It'll be here tomorrow. And every day."

She held him as his breathing quieted.

ten

It soon became apparent that J.R. was temperamentally unlike the other children. His first eagerness to join in was gone; he was content just to exist among them. He was passive, neither wanting nor expecting to play an active role as a full-fledged member of the family. He made it easy for the others to ignore him. He was only slightly older than Phong, two years older than Sunee and Karen, but he had none of their childish enthusiasm. Time after time Dorothy told the younger children, "Get J.R. into whatever you're doing. Don't leave him out of your games. When you're sitting around talking, talk to him, too. You have to remember that he can't see. You'll have to give him directions and help him when you play games. When you leave the room, tell him where you're going and when you'll be back. How is he supposed to know what's going on? You have to use words to help him see and understand what's happening."

She tried to set an example. "Here's your plate, J.R. The hamburger is in the middle, the potato on the right, the vegetable on the left. Your milk is about an inch or so in front of your plate."

Occasionally she absentmindedly continued the description: "Now, here's your plate, Karen. The broccoli is bright green, just like the color of leaves on the trees."

Karen looked up at her and said, "*Mom-mee*, I can see the color."

Dorothy laughed. "All right, so I'm cracking up a little bit. It'll pass."

The children tried, but they quickly forgot her instructions about J.R. More often than not she found the ten-year-old boy slumped apathetically in his chair while his younger sisters were playing Monopoly. He didn't insist on being involved, and the children saw no need to make room for him in their activities. Sometimes they abandoned him in the family room without a word. He didn't seem to mind. He let uncountable hours drift away in daydreams.

One afternoon Dorothy called a conference of the three little girls and Phong. "I've told you about J.R.'s problems, but it hasn't gotten through to you," she announced. "What we're going to do now is this: each one of you is going to take a turn at being blind and not able to walk. You'll be blindfolded and you won't be allowed to use your legs for three hours. That way you'll learn what J.R. is up against."

The children eagerly approved; it sounded like a new game. Sunee was first. She eased herself into the wheelchair and giggled as Dorothy blindfolded her. But she soon was seething with frustration. She and J.R. played Old Maid with braille cards, the boy identifying each card for her. While eating she couldn't locate the food on her plate, couldn't tell if food was falling off the plate. When reaching for her milk, she knocked over the cup. She dropped her napkin, had to grope for it without leaving the chair, and grew angry over her inability to locate it. Dorothy reminded her, "When that happens to J.R., Sunee, you be aware of it and say, 'The napkin is just inside your right wheel,' which is where your napkin is." When Dorothy finally removed the blindfold Sunee said, "Mommy, I see what you mean."

Phong, blindfolded, played braille checkers with J.R. He dropped a checker and, simulating paralyzed legs, slid down from the chair to find it. He groped about for ten minutes in vain, nearly bringing himself to a fit of frustration. The ebullient Wendy did well blindfolded because of her experience with blindness, but she too became furious by her inability to lift herself back into the chair without using her legs.

After Karen seated herself in the chair, she said, "But Mommy, if I can't get out of the chair, I can't go upstairs."

"That's right," Dorothy said. "Neither can J.R. He's a prisoner of the first floor." Karen shook her head sympathetically. At that moment a friend of the family dropped by with three boxed gifts for the younger girls. It took blindfolded Karen several minutes of fumbling with the strings to open her package, which contained a small doll. The child pleaded, "What is it? What is it?"

Dorothy said, "Now you're learning how it is when you can't see. You can't see it, but you can feel it, and that's what J.R. does."

"But Mommy, I can't feel," Karen reminded her.

"Oh, I forgot. It's a little doll, and you can feel it by putting it to your cheek."

Dorothy put herself through the same exercise. She couldn't understand why J.R. couldn't comb his hair neatly. She blindfolded herself, disheveled her hair, and tried to comb it. She had little trouble, but she knew it was not a fair test. After all, she'd been combing her hair for years, while J.R. had never learned how. So she worked with him for a dozen mornings, teaching him how to hold and angle the comb and how to determine with a light, running touch of his fingers whether the hair was neat and the part was straight.

J.R. had never been taught to make his bed, a routine chore for all the other children. Dorothy pulled his bed from the wall to put all four sides within reach. Blindfolded, she sat in a wheelchair and tried to make up the bed. Here, too, she had a strong advantage: she had made beds thousands of times and it was easy for her to visualize the appearance and check neatness by feel. She also had a longer reach than J.R.

But she put him to work on the bed. "All right, J.R., feel the sheet. It's smooth. Now I'll mess it up a bit as if it's been slept on. Smooth it out by pulling on the ends tucked under the mattress. Run your hands over it. There's a big wrinkle, right? If the wrinkle runs across the width of the bed, you can get rid of it by pulling on the sheet at the ends of the bed. If the wrinkle goes down the length, you can smooth it out by pulling the sheet along the sides."

It was too much for the boy. His hand movements were awkward, reluctant, tentative. Dorothy suspended the bed-making project, resumed it again in a week, and kept at it until J.R. could arrange an acceptable-looking bed.

The holiday season meant warmth and love, but it also meant that Dorothy got far behind in her work. AASK required a great deal of time. As the new year started, she suddenly realized the enormous load she and Bob were carrying: household duties, professional duties, immigration and adoption problems. She found

Bob shows Anh and Tich how to transplant vegetables.

Sunee, Dat, Wendy, Karen, Dorothy, and Bob playing ball.

Opposite: Sunee has already shown considerable talent at the piano. Here Melanie stands by to turn the page of music for her.

ANDERS-STERN

Right: The three little girls dance to Dorothy's piano.

A prayer before supper. The children take turns saying grace each night. On the far right is longtime friend and adopted "grandma," Mamie Crocker. Tich, in the doorway, takes all his meals standing up because of problems with pressure sores (1973).

COURTESY SAN FRANCISCO EXAMINER

Karen and Wendy watch as Sunee finishes braiding her pigtails.

ANDERS-STERN

Horseplay in the backyard: Dat, Doni, Phong, Trang, and Bob.

SUSAN ELIZABETH HARRIS

Music is a language the whole family shares in common. Here Noël helps Karen with the marimba.

Bob and Dorothy have just arrived with J.R. for a happy Thanksgiving. Left to right, on porch: Noël, Bob, Dorothy, Mimi, Dat, J.R., Tich, Marty, Karen, Mike, Steffi standing with Wendy and Phong, Doni, Melanie, Kim, Trang; on steps: Sunee and Anh.

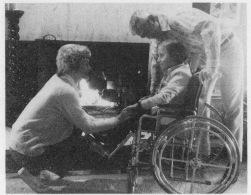

Left: J.R. with Dorothy and Bob in front of the living-room fireplace.

Below: An evening wrestling bout with Bob.

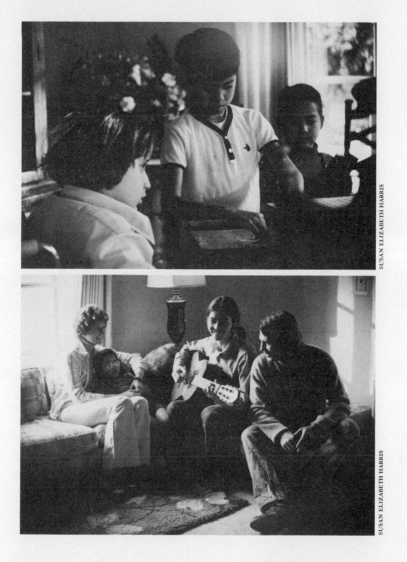

Top: J.R. and Phong play braille Scrabble while Sunee looks on.

Bottom: Mimi, Wendy, Kim, and Mike at the family reunion on Thanksgiving, 1974.

SUSAN ELIZABETH HARRIS

SUSAN ELIZABETH HARRIS

Above: First meeting with Lee in the hospital, May 1975: Bob, Dorothy, Trang, Twe, and Lee.

Opposite: J.R. climbs the "mountain" at last.

Below: Twe too loves music. Here Dorothy and Bob watch her playing the marimba with her fists.

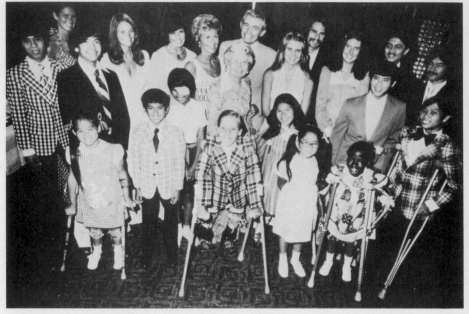

The whole family—so far. The younger children, left to right: Sunee, Phong, Twe, J.R., Lee, Wendy, Karen. Behind them: Trang, Noël, Dat, Stephanie, Mimi, Dorothy, Nana (Bob's mother), Bob, Melanie, Mike, Doni, Anh, Marty, Kim and Tich.

herself yearning for the day the children were back in school, craving solitude so badly that she couldn't stand it. There were too many visitors, too many different hours to keep. Everything the children did seemed to go wrong, to grate her nerves, to end in her screaming at them. She went up to her room, put a big KEEP OUT sign on her door, and sat down to cry. But even in her room, nothing worked right. The check stubs wouldn't balance; the bills wouldn't make sense. Her head was ready to explode. She was desperate for a chance to get away alone with her husband.

They managed to go off by themselves some six or seven times a year, at least for a couple of days—to be husband and wife, together in privacy. That was the only way they could survive. Those short interludes served to fill a reservoir drained dry, to give them the energy to function, to carry them through to the spring vacation when they could get away for two weeks, and leave the children to Nana—Bob's mother, who was ready always to come and care for them. They loved her and enjoyed those spring vacations thoroughly.

Bob understood the depth of Dorothy's need to be alone at times, and so he had given her a special Christmas present. Under the tree she had found twelve gaily wrapped boxes tied together with red ribbon. In each box was a certificate for one twelve-hour day by herself—without husband or children—marked for each month of the year. She had wept with joy at his understanding.

The first twelve-hour period that she had the house to herself, a Sunday, Bob told everyone the night before that he wanted the older ones out of the house by nine A.M. and not back until nine P.M. No coming back for something forgotten. Melanie protested that she needed to change clothes for an afternoon play rehearsal at school, and he suggested that she take her clothes to a girl friend's house. Tich and Anh were to visit friends in Berkeley, Trang relatives in San Francisco.

Bob planned a special treat for the younger ones. They had no television at home—Bob and Dorothy had decided over three years earlier that life in their particular family was better without it—and Bob decided to give them a full day of TV. He called a Holiday Inn, asked to reserve a room for twelve hours, explained he was bringing five children aged six to ten and that they must have a color TV. Then he rounded up a stack of books and games to take along with him the next morning.

The procession of wheelchairs and crutches went through the lobby, into the elevator, and up to the room. Phong, who along with J.R. had never been in a motel before, headed straight for the TV. They started with early morning cartoons, J.R. content to listen to the chatter.

They had been there only half an hour when the bell captain arrived wheeling a cart containing a platter of dozens of homemade cookies, five glasses of milk, and a pot of coffee—compliments of the manager, who had recognized Bob's name and knew about his family. The children had a feast. Lunch was room-service hamburgers, and supper room-service fried chicken.

Bob read to them, and the children took turns reading stories. J.R. read aloud from his braille book.

They played a few games, but primarily they watched television: Phong and J.R. wanted a football game; the little girls didn't. They compromised on fifteen minutes of the game and fifteen of something else.

In the course of the day, J.R. had to have his bag emptied a few times, and Sunee threw up. By the end of the day, Bob was ready to climb a wall or jump out a window. But they got home in one piece and found a restored mother eager to see them. Dorothy had enjoyed a marvelous day. She had taken a long, relaxing soak in a hot bath. She'd played show tunes on the piano, belting out the lyrics. She'd read the papers in a leisurely way and sipped coffee, her feet up. She'd reconciled the checkbook without the slightest difficulty, and written some personal letters. For a full day she had savored the novelty of being alone in a house where the loudest noise was the hum of the refrigerator.

Melanie was wonderfully patient with J.R. It was she who shampooed his hair a couple of times a week, and the two had long conversations. He considered her his friend. And Tich and Anh amiably changed his bag—a procedure that took thirty to forty minutes—without being the least bit resentful. Even if they were going out, they'd get the bag changed first, kidding with the boy as they worked. But all of the children failed to realize how completely J.R. was confined to his household and his backyard. The others could go to a show or a restaurant, could take off for a ride or a walk. But none of them thought of taking J.R. with them. When Bob suggested that Melanie and Doni take J.R. to a movie, they asked how J.R. could possibly see a movie. Bob pointed out that he could hear the show, just as he did TV—and enjoy their company.

Bob and Dorothy took the boy to a children's zoo, and he had a wonderful time holding the baby animals.

Later they put him on the grass in a huge park and told him to wheel around to his heart's content. And he took off in his wheelchair, first tentatively and then delightedly.

By the end of January he was becoming more of a functioning person. He still rarely undertook a new task voluntarily, but he was not only obedient to directions and orders, but responsive to praise. He learned to transfer himself from bed to chair, and back again. He emptied his bedside urinal into the toilet each morning. He completely dressed himself, then wheeled to his place at the kitchen table. After breakfast he carried his dish and utensils to the sink counter and returned to his room to make his bed. He assembled his school materials. Then Bob wheeled him to the curb where they waited for the bus to take him to the California School for the Blind.

J.R.'s ileal conduit bag needed to be changed every two or three days, and Tich and Anh had been trying to teach J.R. to handle the chore. They had had little success. The adhesive-coated ring that held the bag to his lower right abdomen had to be very accurately placed, and doing this depended mostly on vision: it would take J.R. a long time before he could learn to adjust it by feel.

One evening, when the two older boys were out, Bob took over the bag-changing chore. J.R. said, "Dad, there's something I've been wanting to talk to you about." This sentence had become his preamble to a serious talk.

"What's on your mind, J.R.?"

"I don't think I'm going to have any children when I grow up."

"How come?"

"I don't think I could give the discipline that you have to give children."

"Discipline is loving, just as much as kissing or hugging is loving."

"I know. I know you have to teach things to children. But I don't think I can discipline them."

"It has to be done at times. It makes it easier for them to live with themselves and with others."

"I understand. I know that Karen must not wet her bucket. But it would make me feel bad to have to send her alone to her room."

"It doesn't make Mom or me feel good. But Karen has to learn to control that. And she has. It doesn't happen very often. So, the discipline is working."

"I know you're right. But I couldn't do it. I've decided to take the Pill and not have any children."

Bob smiled. "Well, maybe you'll change your mind."

One day in early March J.R. asked his mother, "Will we adopt any more children?"

"I don't know. There's no way to tell. But it wouldn't surprise me if we did. Why do you ask?"

"Well, it's sort of difficult being the last child in a family."

"I suppose it is. Would you want us to adopt again?"

"Oh, yes. That way, there would be somebody that I could help, instead of everybody helping me."

"Hey, J.R., it's so great to hear you say that, but we don't plan adoptions. They just kind of happen. Like that nurse writing to us about you. Who could tell ahead of time that would happen?"

"I see what you mean."

eleven

A FEW WEEKS LATER Dorothy and Bob were awakened at six A.M. by the telephone. It was an acquaintance who worked for the Friends For All Children, a Colorado adoption agency that was heavily involved in bringing foreign orphans to the United States. The situation in Vietnam was critical: the government of Saigon was about to fall. A children's airlift was being organized. "I have a cable from Phyllis Kaplan," she said excitedly. "She's in Saigon. She has two orphans, a blind thirteen-year-old and a paralyzed fourteen-year-old, who might be helped by surgery. She can get them out of Vietnam on medical visas if adoptive families are guaranteed. She has to have an answer immediately. Do you have families ready and willing?" Dr. Kaplan, a child psychologist, was familiar with the DeBolt family and the efforts of AASK.

Bob repeated the message to his wife and they exchanged a long look.

"Tell her she's got the family," Bob told the woman.

"For both children?"

"Yes. We will adopt them."

There was a long moment of silence from the other end. Then the woman said, in a tone that sounded a little incredulous, "Well, thank you, Bob. And thank Dorothy. I'll send off a cable right away."

For several minutes Dorothy and Bob were silent. They had just bought tickets for two new adventures. They pictured, during the course of these trips, a blind child given vision and a paralyzed child given the ability to walk and climb the staircase to the second floor. This was the hope, the dream, the reason for being alive.

As usual the children took the news enthusiastically. J.R. was especially pleased. "Maybe I'll be able to help the blind child. It would really make me feel good to help a child."

But the DeBolts heard nothing more about the two children until April 3 when Dr. Kaplan landed at San Francisco and telephoned Dorothy. "Your two children should be here soon," she reported. "I met both at the Allambie Orphanage in Saigon. The blind child is a thirteen-year-old girl by the name of Twe. At the orphanage she sat in a corner and rocked back and forth. I was told that she was mentally retarded. I found nothing of the kind. She wasn't making contact with other people because she had been ignored, discarded, deprived.

"The other girl is Ly. Paralyzed from the waist down—polio, I guess. I found her in the same orphanage, getting around on a kind of skateboard. She wore slippers on her hands to push herself. Yet she was a great one for helping the younger children. She saw a lot of them leave the place. She dreamed about being one of them.

"Your children should be flying here as part of a large group. I'm going to the Presidio now where the children will be received. Fifty-two arrived today. God knows how many will be flown out. Many hundreds. People are working like crazy in Saigon to get the kids out before the government collapses."

On the following day Dorothy and Bob drove to the Presidio to volunteer their help. The cavernous training hall at the military base had been hastily converted to a reception center for the arriving children. Volunteer groups in the Bay Area had provided hundreds of mattresses, blankets, toys, teething rings, and diapers, as well as food for the children, and some two hundred doctors, nurses, adoption agency workers, immigration authorities, and local women had offered to care for the children. Two planeloads had arrived. Pediatricians had climbed into the aircraft to check the children and sent the most seriously ill directly to hospitals by ambulance. The others, about 90 percent, went to the Presidio by bus. There, many needed to be treated for pneumonia, measles, chicken pox, diarrhea, ear infections, skin diseases, scabies and lice. After medical examinations and, if necessary, treatment, the children were processed by immigration officials and adoption workers, then picked up by adoptive parents. Other planes with children were en route to Seattle and New York City.

Dorothy and Bob were assigned to handle press relations, and to find families, through AASK, for any handicapped children who did not yet have them. Between news bulletins and answering questions they fed and diapered infants and tried to comfort the frightened older children.

Neither of their girls was on the arrival lists.

About one o'clock on Saturday morning they heard the appalling news of the crash of the C-5A military transport that was carrying 243 orphans and some sixty men and women. The plane had hardly started gaining altitude after takeoff from the airport outside Saigon when a cargo door blew out, causing depressurization and the crash. Some 150 children and fifty adults were killed.

The tragedy numbed the volunteers at the Presidio. Dorothy and Bob reacted to its enormity with silent shock. Phyllis Kaplan sat next to Dorothy on a mattress. "Many children from Allambie were scheduled to be on that flight," she said, her voice breaking. They sat silently as Dorothy rocked a baby in her arms.

After working until three A.M. Dorothy and Bob drove home. At dinner that night the whole family said a prayer for Twe and Ly and the other children on the fatal flight.

Shortly after midnight an adoptions worker telephoned from the Presidio. "Dorothy, your blind daughter arrived! She was on the plane that crashed, but she wasn't even injured. Miraculous! We don't know about your other daughter. We think she was on the same plane. She apparently survived, but that's all we have."

Dorothy let out a whoop of joy and shouted the news through the house. After a few tears Melanie said, "I'll get her bed ready."

Bob said, "Okay, now all you smaller children, back to bed. Mom and I will pick up Twe and be back in a couple hours."

Tich, Anh, and Trang asked if they could go along to do the interpreting. Bob told them to hurry into clothes. J.R. wheeled himself back to his room, and Melanie shepherded the other children to their rooms.

Dr. Kaplan greeted the family as they entered the reception hall, grabbed Dorothy's hand, and led them to an improvised playroom. She pointed to a girl being guided between mattresses by a volunteer. Dorothy approached the child, who wore thongs on her feet and walked duck-footed, toes pointed outward. Her chin virtually touched her chest, as if she were trying to hide her face. Dorothy said, "Twe." The thirteen-year-old turned her head, showing one eye deeply sunken and atrophied and the other abnormally large and covered by a thick film. The child tried an uneasy smile. Dorothy embraced her. The smile abruptly disappeared and Twe pushed Dorothy's arms away.

After she was examined by a physician, the family led her to the car. The first sound of the motor and the movement of the car obviously frightened her; she told the boys that it felt like an airplane. During the drive home Dorothy attempted to touch her several times but she always withdrew or pushed away the hand. Even an accidental touch by one of the boys provoked the same reaction. The boys tried to draw her into conversation. After a few exchanges Tich told Dorothy and Bob, "She thinks that she came to America to get her eyes fixed. She hopes God lets her open her eyes. I don't think she understands about being adopted. She can't remember anything about her family. She must have been given to the orphanage when she was pretty young."

They reached home about four A.M. After getting Twe settled and giving Tich, Anh, and Melanie some instructions about running the household and making certain that the younger children left for school on time, Dorothy and Bob drove back to the Presidio to continue their work. Planes with children kept arriving, but no information about Ly was available. After two days of working with the news media and caring for children, two days in which they caught only a few hours of sleep at a nearby motel, Dorothy and Bob returned home.

Twe was sullen and hostile. She wanted to be left alone. She hated to be touched. She struck out, sometimes so violently that she dug scratches in any hand that attempted to be friendly. She sat on her haunches, rocking back and forth. Sometimes, when addressed, she covered her face and cowered.

She couldn't understand why Dorothy kept reaching for her by touch and expression. She apparently had never known personal affection. One morning Dorothy complimented her, "Twe, you look pretty."

"No pretty!" Twe violently protested. "No pretty!" Later Tich told Dorothy that the girl had asked him about the comment and said, "Americans are crazy. They think I'm pretty. I wonder why they say that. In Vietnam I was ugly."

During the first few days at the house she wanted to eat by raising the plate to her chin and shoving the food by hand into her mouth, then wiping her hand on her dress or the table. She was fascinated by the bathroom faucets. After feeling her way from the bedroom shared with Melanie to the bathroom, she stood before the sink, kept filling a glass with water, and poured the tumbler over her head until her hair, pajamas, and slippers were sopping. After being taught to use a washcloth she washed herself time after time. Water in any amount desired seemed an unbelievable luxury.

Gradually, the family and the house became familiar to her. The boys had told her that she now was a member of the family with the same rights as any other child. She allowed Dorothy to take her hand and guide her to the various contents of the kitchen's drawers and cabinets. She said, "Good morning," as she groped her way into the kitchen for breakfast. She smiled when Bob greeted her by name.

Dorothy soon discovered that she loved music and taught her to operate the record player in the family room. She sat for hours, rocking to the rhythm of children's songs and softly singing along with the vocalists. Sunee, Karen and Wendy often joined her. They learned to sing the chorus of each song and to allow her to do the solo of the verse.

Five days after the crash Dr. Kaplan got through to the Allambie Orphanage and was told that Ly had been in the plane accident and had suffered internal bleeding and four leg fractures. She had been placed in a body cast and was being treated at the Seventh Day Adventist Hospital in Saigon.

Since the fall of the South Vietnamese government appeared imminent, the DeBolts were anxious to get Lee (they had decided that this spelling would be preferable) to the States as quickly as possible. They telephoned the orphanage supervisor and urged her to try to get Lee on a flight. The woman told Dorothy that Lee had incurred a bone infection and would need medical supervision during the flight. Dorothy pleaded with her to try to get the child on a military hospital evacuation flight.

They heard nothing about the child for nearly three weeks. Then, on May 1, an adoptions worker at Travis Air Force Base near San Francisco reported that Lee had arrived on a refugee flight from Guam and was safe at the base hospital. That evening Bob arranged to have her transferred by ambulance to the Children's Hospital in Oakland.

Dorothy had Anh ask Twe if she knew Lee. "Yes, I liked her," the girl said. "Is she with the other children in the crash who went to Heaven and are living with God?"

Dorothy told her that Lee was alive, but injured, and that she could visit her friend on the following day. She didn't mention that Lee would be her sister. She wanted both girls to be together to hear the news.

Trang went with them to the hospital to meet the new sister, just a year younger than he. Dorothy guided Twe's hand to Lee's cheek. Lee said, "Twe," and both girls embraced. Lee took a cross on a light silver chain from around her neck and handed it to Dorothy, indicating that she wanted it placed around Twe's neck. Trang then explained to Lee that Dorothy and Bob would be her parents, and that she and Twe would be sisters in the same house. The girls burst into excited conversation. Trang told Dorothy and Bob, "They're pretty mixed up about all this. It'll take a little time to straighten out. But they both feel happy about being together."

Lee told Trang that she had become paralyzed at the age of three. She was eight when her mother died. A year later her father was caught in a combat zone and disappeared, and her uncle placed her in an orphanage. She was transferred from the orphanage in Da Nang to one in Saigon, where she and Twe were the oldest children.

Eleven days later, the black-haired, broad-faced girl came home to the second floor bedroom she shared with Melanie and Twe. She was still in a cast and so had to be carried up and down the stairs; whoever was available did bedpan duty.

The hospital nurses had told the DeBolts that Lee

didn't like American food. She was a problem eater who preferred only rice. On her first evening at home the older boys cooked a Vietnamese dinner that she obviously enjoyed. The next morning Dorothy served French toast. Lee took one bite and left the remainder. Dorothy nodded at Tich and said, "Give Lee the house eating rules."

Tich explained that everyone in the family ate the same food and everyone ate what was put before them. "No way to change that, sister," he concluded. Lee considered the words. She asked him if *nuoc mang* was available. This was a Vietnamese sauce, almost as hot as tabasco, that was commonly sprinkled over fish, meats, and vegetables. Tich and Anh always had a jar of the homemade sauce on hand. Lee doused the French toast with it. For several weeks, until her palate adjusted, she poured *nuoc mang* on all food, including cornflakes.

Before taking Twe for an eye examination, Dorothy had Anh explain to her that there was no certainty that the physician would be able to give her vision. He had been able to help Wendy, but not J.R. Several examinations would be required to determine if an operation was feasible for Twe.

When Dorothy and Twe got home from the doctor that July afternoon with the news that Twe had a good chance of regaining vision in one eye, all the family gathered in the kitchen while the lamb casserole and Bob's zucchini dish finished baking in the oven. Wendy's daisies were in the middle of the table.

"Make sure she understands, boys," Dorothy said to Tich and Anh. "Tell her it's not one hundred percent. But tell her the doctors think there's a good chance."

Anh relayed the information in rapid Vietnamese. Twe nodded, a shy smile on her pretty face, and briefly responded. Anh said, "She understand. She feel very happy about it."

J.R. said, "It's great, Twe. You'll be able to learn English much faster." J.R. had been coaching her in English for several weeks.

When the dinner was ready and the family was seated, Dorothy said, "Wendy, would you like to say grace?" Everybody held hands.

Wendy lowered her head and said, "Thank you, God, for my mother and father and brothers and sisters. Thank you for wanting to help Twe's eye. Thank you for the food on this table. . . ." She paused, thinking. "And for the daisies too. Amen."

twelve

Less than a month after that day in July 1975, the opthalmologist transplanted a cornea into Twe's eye. Three days later Dorothy and Trang watched him and a nurse cut away the bandages around Twe's head. "The transplant may not have taken," the doctor warned. "We'll just have to see." He shone a very bright light into the eye and told Trang, "Ask her if she sees the light."

After several exchanges with Twe, Trang said, "She asks, what is light?"

The doctor moved the thin, glaring beam back and forth across the eye. "That's good," he said. "Her eye followed it. There is a chance. Tell her that light is what she just saw."

While Twe was hospitalized Bob got Lee fitted with braces and crutches. He drove her home, carried her up the front steps and stood her up in the hall. He was confident that walking and climbing would be no problem for her. She was strong and wiry. She had openly envied the walking ability of the other children, kept asking when she would be braced, and gave no indication of fear. She wanted to walk: she *would* walk.

Lee jiggled and wobbled a little as she first tried to

gain her balance, then she began moving her crutches forward and dragging her feet. Within a few hours she had shifted to a short, tentative swing-through gait. That first night she climbed the stairs to her room.

On Twe's return from the hospital three days later Lee immediately assumed responsibility for applying drops to the younger girl's eye six times a day and making certain that the eye shield was firmly attached to the face at bedtime.

Twe's vision developed very slowly. She perceived light and dark, but small objects usually were an unrecognizable blur to her. The family kept checking and testing her vision. While they were playing in the yard, Phong held up a beachball. Twe cocked her head, trying to focus on the object, and finally said, "Round. Ball. Blue color." But her ability was erratic. An hour later she couldn't see the ball. Dorothy watched the child turn away in frustration and disappointment. Dorothy reached for her hand and said, "Try to be patient, honey."

Twe nodded. "How long it take Wendy to see?" she asked.

Dorothy explained that it took Wendy's vision a year to develop fully. She wanted to avoid either encouraging or discouraging the child. "The doctors will do all they can, Twe. We can only hope."

"Yes, hope," Twe said. "I hope."

Three months after the operation a cataract began forming over Twe's eye, and her vision was limited to light and shadow. The doctor did not consider it a major problem, and he planned to deal with it when he removed the stitches in the transplant in early 1976. Meanwhile Twe was admitted to the school for the blind that J.R. attended.

In mid-January—seven months after her arrival in this country—Lee was enrolled in the seventh grade at Piedmont Junior High. She had long since assumed a place in the family, exercising a mild parental-type authority over the younger children, voluntarily doing more than her share of work, mending clothes and sewing hems. She was energetic and ambitious as well, and she learned English quickly. It was this that made it possible for her to enter school sooner than anyone anticipated.

The attitudes that inspired Lee and others in the family—ambition and hope—were somehow missing in J.R. He had gotten just so far and no farther. He seemed reconciled to remaining forever bound to his wheelchair, accepting it as stoically as he had accepted the verdict about his eyes—that the optic nerve was destroyed and he would never see again.

The DeBolts had been convinced that a permanent sitting position did not have to be this boy's future. "J.R., you can walk," Bob had told him. "From the waist down, you're no different from Sunee or Karen or Tich or Anh. And you know how they get around. It's just a matter of work. Hard work. You have to build up those arm and shoulder muscles. They'll do the work of your legs. They'll support your body. You can do it. And when you do it, every one of us is going to be proud of you, but no one is going to be more proud than you are."

The boy was visibly inspired. "Yes, Dad. I'll do my best. I will. If the other children can do it, why can't I." It was a statement, not a question.

So each afternoon Bob, Tich, or Anh had drilled J.R. on sit-ups, rollovers, pushups, and barbell exercises. He had obediently gone through the motions, but he had not exhibited any conviction about the training. It was as if he doubted that strength would enable him to walk.

Bob had decided to put the responsibility for exercises entirely on the boy. "From now on, J.R., you do the exercises on your own. You don't need us standing over you. You know what to do. So do them because you understand what they're going to do for you."

J.R. continued to perform without conviction. He didn't work or strain. He showed no desire to make an effort. Sometimes, during exercise periods or when he was not engaged with others, he retreated into a private world. It was obvious to Bob when J.R. "left." The boy slowly turned his head, smiled, frowned, moved his lips. Finally, Bob asked, "What are you doing, J.R.?"

"Oh, nothing."

"It seemed to me that you were imagining yourself doing something."

"Yes, that's true. I was on a boat going to Europe."

"Well, that sounds like a pleasant trip. We all have our fantasies, but it's bad if we spend too much time at them. It wastes time. It's a way of avoiding what we should be doing. You must never start dreaming, J.R., during exercise sessions. And when you're just sitting I want you to be working on your braille cards—the arithmetic, spelling, and sentence cards."

"All right, Dad."

After J.R. had been exercising for several weeks, Bob got him into his braces. He wanted him to adjust to the weight and feel of the braces during the routine of the day. Each day Bob buckled them over the shoes and up the legs and tightly strapped the corset that supported the lower back. He waited for the boy to assist him. Finally J.R. reached down, felt for a strap, and buckled it around his thigh. "Just did you a favor, Dad," he pointed out.

"No favor to me," Bob retorted. "You did a favor for yourself. You were helping yourself. What pleases Mom and me is when you do things for yourself—when you do something today that you weren't able to do yesterday. From now on you do the braces yourself. It'll take you quite a while at first, but be patient. Don't ask for help simply because it's easier for someone to do it for you."

J.R. met that challenge, and gradually he learned to manage the arduous chore by himself.

It was April when Bob held J.R. upright on his braces and Tich slipped crutches under his armpits. The boy stood there, frightened, quivering, his crutches shaking. For the first time in his eleven years he was vertical, supported only by crutches. Bob and the boys tried to cajole him into movement, but he was immobilized. Bob held his shoulders. Tich and Anh moved his feet between the crutches, then advanced the crutch tips a few inches. Since he couldn't see, they tried to get him to feel the rhythm of the swing-through gait.

J.R. couldn't do it. His muscles still lacked the strength to control and maneuver his body. He couldn't maintain his balance. He slumped on the crutches, letting the armpit crossbars support his entire weight. Day after day his instructors hammered away at him.

"Stiffen your arms, J.R.!"

"Get your armpits off those crutches! How are you going to move the crutches if all your weight is on them?"

"Straighten up! Straighten up!"

Bob made J.R. do pushups on the crutches, tightening his fists on the lower rungs and straightening his arms so that his weight was carried by his arms and shoulders. The boy gradually achieved thirty pushups, but he let his weight fall on the crutches when he moved or when Bob wasn't standing nearby.

Finally, after a barrage of encouragement and goading, J.R. began moving. He placed his left crutch a few inches forward. Leaning on it he slid the right crutch to a parallel position. Then he dragged both feet between the crutches. It took him a minute to travel a foot. But there was no desire, no internal push. J.R. moved because he was told to move. Something was missing in him. He seemed to lack the heart to fight. He felt neither the need nor the desire to become more proficient, able, and independent.

They had tried to use the other children as examples for him to emulate. They had tried praise and encouragement. They had tried direct orders. Bob took another approach one evening. "I've got an idea," he told the boy. "Mother's Day is two weeks away. What do you think of this surprise for Mom? On Mother's Day you walk from the library, through the front hall and kitchen, and into your bedroom. You go up to your bed, let go of the crutches, and drop onto the bed. All on your own."

J.R. was enthusiastic. He practiced and worked with Bob, Tich, and Anh when Dorothy was upstairs in her bedroom or out of the house. Bob rehearsed him on landmarks so that he could make the trip without verbal guidance. He would brush against a large potted plant as he left the library. His left crutch would strike the first step of the staircase, putting him on a course through the kitchen entrance. As he moved into the kitchen he would be able to feel a small table on his left, at which point he would turn left turn down the length of the kitchen. He could guide himself by keeping his left forearm near the edge of the cooking island counter. He memorized the number of steps through the small hallway between the kitchen and his bedroom. Then he was only about 6 feet from his bed which he could feel with a crutch. It was a grueling, tedious journey. But J.R. didn't balk or quit. Sweating and huffing, he grimly traversed the route with dragging feet.

On Mother's Day he told Dorothy, "I have a present for you." He slowly hauled himself along the practiced route. At the end, when he dropped his crutches and flopped on the bed, Dorothy sprawled beside him and hugged him and cried her appreciation for his gift.

The following week Bob suggested to J.R. that he try various routes through the house. In the course of these excursions he could memorize the positions of furniture in each room and learn the crutch distance between objects and between rooms. Bob described a circuitous route to his place at the kitchen table as his first venture.

"Fine," said J.R. "What's this for?"

"It's good practice. It'll make you more comfortable and confident in getting through the house."

"I mean, who is this for?"

"It's for you, buddy boy."

"Can't I do it for somebody?"

"Well, Steffi will be home in a week or so. She's never seen you on crutches, and it'll be a big surprise to her."

"Do you think she'll cry?"

Bob didn't like the question. J.R.'s attitude was wrong if he considered his walking a performance to evoke a sentimental response. "Steffi doesn't need to cry to show appreciation for your progress," Bob said. "I know that she'll be very happy for you."

After J.R. displayed his ability for Steffi, Bob outlined a new route.

"What is this one for?" J.R. asked. "What's the occasion?"

"It's for you to get off your butt," Bob replied with some irritation. "It's for you to walk like everybody else. It's for you to be able to do more for yourself. What can be a more special occasion than your being able to get around?" Bob couldn't understand why J.R. didn't *want* to walk.

J.R. impassively listened to the reprimand. He showed neither hurt nor anger. He slowly dragged his feet toward his bedroom.

Through the weeks Bob and the older boys kept urging him to lift his armpits off the crutches. They had little success. One morning in June Bob told J.R to extend his right hand to touch a doorjamb as a guide. J.R. reached. His hand hung limply from the wrist. Bob said, "You can touch more easily if you straighten out your hand, J.R.."

"I can't."

Bob knew then that there was nerve involvement from the pressure of the crutches against the armpits. "Can you make a fist?"

The boy tried. "No."

"When did this start?"

"A few days ago."

"You should have told us."

"Well, Mom and you don't like me to complain, so I didn't think I should say anything."

"We don't like complaints about how hard walking is or about doing your chores. But your health is a different matter. Telling us about illness or pain or something happening to your hand isn't complaining. It's important for us to know. We want to know."

"Okay, Dad."

"Now, no more crutches until that hand comes back. You'll have to stay in the chair or on the floor. But you must go right ahead each day with your exercises. About your hand—Tich and Anh have a hand exerciser, a gadget with two handles that you squeeze like a ball. You squeeze that thing every minute you can."

A neurologist examined J.R.'s hand and found that two nerves had been damaged. He recommended exercises: the squeezer, spreading and closing the fingers, continual effort to keep the hand extended on a straight line from the forearm and vigorous pounding of piano keys. But he could give no assurance that the exercises would induce the return of normal nerve function.

Bob told Dorothy what the neurologist said, then added, "I'm convinced we can get that hand back to normal—but only if J.R. works at it. And he isn't going to do the work on his own. I don't think he's even upset about losing power in that hand. We have to *demand* that he exercise, and no fooling around about it."

"Yes, let's get tough with him," Dorothy agreed. "But we've got to let him know that we're being tough because we love him. That if we didn't care about him it wouldn't matter to us whether he stayed in that chair for the rest of his life. We've got to find some way to motivate him."

During the following week Dorothy and Bob were busy fund raising for AASK and addressing meetings concerned with adoptions. They were involved in converting the AASK chapter in Nevada to a state-approved adoption service that would conduct home studies of families that wanted to adopt handicapped children. In the fourteen months of AASK's existence homes had been found for more than two hundred children with special needs—deaf, blind, mongoloid, paralyzed—but home studies and approval of these adoptions were still handled by each family's local licensed adoption agency. The adoption process often was very slow; the Nevada program was a first effort at reducing the delay in bringing together child and family.

Whenever they had the opportunity, Dorothy and Bob tried to correct a misunderstanding that was prevalent among the organizations AASK solicited for support and among the parents contemplating adoption: that they had unlimited funds of their own, and that you had to be rich to do what they were doing. Anyone who lived in that big house at that Piedmont address with that many children must be exceptionally well off, outsiders reasoned. This was not the case. Financially, Dorothy and Bob were not in a position to contribute anything beyond their own time and energy to AASK. They had to rely on the tax-deductible gifts of others to keep the organization functioning. They managed their large household by living carefully, keeping expenses down, asking each child to help with his or her own support within the limits of their individual capabilities. Dorothy's lecture fees provided an important and necessary supplement to their income; and, too, many of the exceptional expenses associated with the care of the handicapped children were borne by such organizations as the Crippled Children Services.

It was false to assume that if you quadrupled the number of children in your household, you quadrupled your costs as well. And people who felt they couldn't "afford" even one more child were more often than not wrong. It was heartbreaking to Dorothy and Bob to realize that so many children were denied families because of such assumptions, and one of their chief objectives was, through AASK, to give the picture as it really was.

J.R. himself was living proof of the need for AASK. The child had been released for adoption at birth, yet no one had adopted him. He was what society tends to consider unadoptable, a throwaway child, and this attitude had placed him in a kind of limbo for years. In a series of foster home situations, he had not consistently received the prompt medical attention that just might have prevented his total blindness at the age of five. It was this kind of tragedy that Dorothy and Bob wanted so passionately to prevent.

Dorothy told J.R. to take the hand exerciser with him when he went to the backyard each morning. "It would be good if you always carried it with you in the wheelchair seat," she said. "That way, when you're doing nothing else with that hand, you can always squeeze it. No miracle is going to make that hand come back, J.R. Only work will do it."

J.R. said, "Sure, Mom, I'll do that."

Late in the morning she glanced through the bedroom window and saw the boy slumped in his chair. He wasn't talking or playing with the other children and he wasn't squeezing the exerciser. He was daydreaming. Twenty minutes later she checked him again: his position and attitude hadn't changed. She asked Trang to bring him into the house. She wheeled him into the foyer and asked, "J.R. have you been doing your sit-ups and pushups and other exercises when we've not been here?"

"I haven't done those for a long time."

"Well, get going on them, right now. And work, J.R. Exercise is a waste of time if you don't work at it. I want to hear you grunt and groan."

The boy slid down from the chair, lay back, and began a sit-up.

Dorothy went to the basement to move laundry from the washer to the dryer. When she returned J.R. was sitting slumped. He was off in space again. She watched him for more than a minute. He didn't move. "What are you supposed to be doing, J.R.?" she said in a level, cold tone.

"Sit-ups."

"Why?"

"To build up my strength."

"Why?"

"So I can walk on braces and crutches."

"Why?"

"So I can get around and do more things," he said quietly.

"Why?" She was deliberately trying to irritate him. She wanted some expression of feeling to burst spontaneously from him.

But he didn't respond. He just turned his head from side to side.

"Are you exercising for you or us?" she demanded.

He didn't answer.

"What difference does it make to us whether or not you walk? It isn't going to change our lives, is it? Answer me."

"No."

"Would it change your life?"

"Yes."

"How?"

"I could do more things."

"But you don't want to do more things, do you, J.R.? You like sitting in a chair like a blob and having people wait on you like they did in the foster homes and the hospitals. You don't want to get up and walk. That's work. You'd rather sit there. It's easier. You think there's always going to be somebody around to help you and wait on you and take care of you? Forget it! It isn't going to be that way. We've never had anybody in this house or this family who just sits around and won't help himself. And we're not going to have it now because it won't work out. Your Dad and I aren't going to be around here forever. What happens when we're not here and you want to get something to eat or go to the bathroom or you've got to reach for something or you've got to get out of the house? What happens then if you're just a blob in a wheelchair?"

"Nothing."

"Right, nothing. Nothing is what you'll be able to do and nothing is what you will be. We can't stand seeing you become that. We want you to get mad at the fact that you're in that wheelchair. We want you to prove to yourself that you don't have to be in that chair.

"It can be done. Look at Tich and Anh. When they arrived here I had to carry Tich in my arms and help both of them with most things, even bowel movements. Look at them now. They can do anything. They're proud of themselves. When they were building themselves up, they lifted weights until they were ready to keel over. I had to tell them to stop. Have I ever had to tell you to stop exercising? No, sir."

J.R. now wore a dazed, bewildered, overwhelmed expression.

224

"Get mad, J.R. Say, 'Listen, lady, you can't call me a blob. I'll show you I can do anything I want to do. Walk, climb stairs, go anywhere in this house that I want to go. I can become strong. I can do it.' "

Dorothy paused. She was breathing heavily. "We love you, J.R.," she said, her voice softer. "We want so much for you to do all the things that you're capable of doing. But we cannot and will not do them for you. You're the guy that's going to have to do them. And nothing will happen until you make up your mind that you are going to do them. The people in this house and in the world will just pass you by. Don't let that happen. You can stay with them, step for step."

She was spent. She waited for a response. None came. He seemed crushed by the attack. "All right, J.R.?" she asked softly.

"All right, Mom," he said in a dull tone.

The following day, she kept checking the boy's activities. He was unusually quiet and withdrawn. He did no sit-ups or pushups. Once she saw him with his right arm extended, spreading and closing the fingers—but indifferently, without exertion. She said nothing. What more could she say? What would stimulate this child? What would keep him from becoming a lifelong chair-bound "patient" in the house?

Bob was growing increasingly impatient with J.R. "I wish I could plug him into an electrical outlet and shock him into a little activity once in a while," he told Dorothy.

"This is all a new way of life for J.R., and I feel kind of sorry for him," Dorothy said. "No one before us has ever given him a rough time. No one has insisted that he fight. No one ever made him feel a need to struggle for his own good."

"I feel sorry for him, too, but a lot of good that does."

"We'll keep working on him. We don't have much choice."

J.R. loved to go to the backyard with the other children after breakfast. He found the sunshine soothing, and he invariably removed his shirt and turned his face to the sun: "It feels nice to get a good tan."

Dorothy decided to make the backyard a privilege. "You'd better devote the morning to exercises, J.R. After you exercise—really exercise—then you can go out and play with the kids in the backyard."

J.R. obediently wheeled himself to the piano. Dorothy heard the light tinkle of two keys. She walked into the family room, J.R. was barely striking the keys in a rocking motion with his thumb and little finger. One look told her that he wasn't really at the piano. He had flown to fantasy-land. Anger swept her. "J.R., you're not doing a damn thing for your fingers that way! Hit those keys! Use all your fingers! Spread your fingers. Force them to do what they don't want to do. You heard the sound your fingers made. Now listen to the sound I make!" She pounded the keys as if she wanted to break them. "See? Hard!" She took each of his fingers and punched them at the keys. Over and over, for ten minutes, she pushed at the keys with his fingers. "Get it, J.R.? Work! The more you force your fingers, the stronger your hand will get. Now, you do it, J.R."

She strode off to the kitchen to make a casserole for dinner. As she cut up vegetables she listened to the piano. Suddenly she stopped working. Something had happened. J.R. was *pounding* the keys.

Later she watched him in the front hall, trying to

do sit-ups. He didn't raise his trunk very far, but he obviously was trying. He was clenching his teeth with the effort. It was the first time she had seen that kind of strain. "Hey! That looks pretty good," she praised him. "You're putting out."

"Yes. Thank you. I'm trying." He continued his exercises in the afternoon. She noted that he was actually working with the barbell. Instead of a lackadaisical raising and lowering of the weight he was jerking it up and down with crispness and snap. Something had obviously stirred him into action.

After J.R. had put on his pajamas that night, Dorothy sat on the bed beside him. "You worked today, J.R.," she said. "It was good to see that. So good."

"I've been thinking about that little speech you gave me."

"That little speech? Oh, you mean when I yelled at you?"

"Yes."

"I hope it made some sense. Did thinking about it make you do those good exercises today?"

"Yes, it did. What you told me was on my mind."

She decided to ask no more questions. It was enough that the lecture produced results. But she wondered precisely what had motivated the boy. She told Bob about J.R.'s change of attitude, and he speculated, "Maybe J.R. inferred a threat—if he didn't shape up we'd send him back to Blythedale."

"I didn't intend that. But if that's what he made of it and if that's what got him moving—fine."

J.R. continued to work with zeal and determination. He pounded the piano keys with all the fingers of his right hand. He clenched the hand exerciser until his arm and hand quivered from the effort. He lifted the barbell until he was exhausted. He did sit-ups until he truly could not raise his shoulders from the floor one more time.

His hand stopped hanging limply from the wrist. Bob tested his grip every few days with a handshake and found it growing progressively stronger. Within a few weeks its strength matched the left hand. The once-damaged nerves were functioning normally.

The total effort made the boy lose weight. His midsection grew flat and hard. Flabby fat disappeared from his arms. His shoulders, which had resembled those of a plump girl, turned firm and muscular.

At the end of August he quickly wheeled into the kitchen and cried, "Mom! Mom, I want to show you something!" He slid from the seat to the floor. Then he pulled himself up the chair and swiveled back into the seat. He had lifted his entire weight with his arms and shoulders, and he was radiant with pride.

Dorothy hugged him, exclaiming, "Terrific! Wait until Dad sees that."

What Bob saw convinced him that J.R. was ready, physically and emotionally, to walk. He had the boy fitted with Canadian crutches, extending only to 2 inches below the elbows and held to the forearms by horseshoe-shaped bands. There was no armpit cross-piece on which J.R. could sag. Balance and walking would depend on strength and confidence.

J.R. was not the least dismayed by the challenge. "Can we start as soon as we get home?" he asked Bob.

"No reason not to. The sooner you go running around the house, the better. But first we have an appointment at the orthodontist to check your teeth."

As they drove home J.R. said, "Dad, the tech-

228

nician at the office kept calling me 'sweetheart.' It made me feel kind of bad. You keep telling me that I have to do things for myself and learn to do things. I think I'm trying and I feel good when I try. 'Sweetheart' was the word they called me at my last foster home. All I ever did there was to sit and be a sweetheart."

Bob groped for words. "Well, those sweetheart days are over. Your old foster parents wouldn't recognize you now." He felt a sorrow and an anger: sorrow for the child who had been abandoned as a human being capable of change and development, and anger with the foster parents who chose to keep him dependent on them rather than stimulating him toward any self-sufficiency.

J.R. was an eager, awkward, resolute pupil on the Canadian crutches. The first problem was balance. He kept falling into Bob's arms. Finally, Bob said, "Let's get Tich and Anh to teach you to fall. If you know how to fall without hurting yourself you'll be more confident about walking. Also, most of the time when you'll be walking, there won't be anyone within range to catch you."

Tich and Anh taught J.R. to fall in the same fashion that they had trained Sunee. And J.R. proved an apt, fearless pupil.

Then, night after night, Bob and the boys worked on J.R.'s walking. The other children hovered nearby, offering encouragement. When he progressed from dragging his feet to lifting them in a short free swing they cheered.

The attitude of the younger children toward J.R. had changed. He was no longer a body in a chair. They developed respect for him. He had lost much of his meekness and submissiveness, had become more assertive. Accomplishment had given him a sense of self-esteem that he had never experienced. He spoke to the younger children with authority. Previously, Phong had ignored him. It was easy: J.R.'s personality never commanded attention. Now the two boys were friends. On most evenings Phong visited J.R.'s room, where they played cards, talked, and listened to the baseball games on the radio. Frequently J.R. read stories from his braille books to Phong.

Dorothy and Bob kept looking for ways to strengthen J.R.'s image among the children. One afternoon, when the boy was exercising in the front hall, the mother and father were in the kitchen scolding Wendy for having helped herself to some brownies Melanie had made. Wendy loved to eat, especially starches and sweets. Dorothy and Bob called her their walking wastebasket. Unless they watched her diet, she would get too fat. So she was under orders never to take sweets between meals. But the worst part was that she'd been sneaky. To Dorothy, that was like lying—being dishonest—which was completely unacceptable in the family. Dorothy scolded her loudly enough for J.R. to hear. "Wendy, J.R. is around here by himself often and he probably loves to eat even more than you do, but he never snitched food. You'd never see him take anything. Why don't you talk to him and find out how he controls himself? J.R.! Did you hear that?"

"Yes, Mom. I think it might help Wendy if I talked to her," he said in his best wise-old-man manner.

Dorothy nodded to Wendy and the girl walked into the hall, contrite, head lowered. Dorothy and Bob eavesdropped shamelessly.

J.R. eagerly took to his task. "Too much sugar is bad for your health and your teeth," he lectured. "I know. Remember how fat I was? That's why I don't eat sweets anymore." Then he said, in the most morally upright tone he could muster, "As for sneakiness, that is something that should never be put up with. You should never sneak. I never sneak cookies—because I can't see where they put them."

Dorothy and Bob ran out of earshot to laugh.

By the end of October J.R. was on braces and crutches around the house. He used the chair only to attend classes at the California School for the Blind in nearby Berkeley. Now he saw the chair as a conveyance for people unable to walk. It was a matter of pride for him not to use it. Mike and Marty had been home late in August and had hardly recognized the boy. He was so much better looking, his whole attitude had changed, and he was now a vital cog in the family. Their pride and pleasure in him and his own happiness in showing himself to them were beautiful for Dorothy to watch. Here was her first-born son Mike, whom some might expect to resent the adopted children; here was her first adopted son Marty, who also might feel deprived by the advent of others; and here was the adopted child who had been the most severely handicapped of the whole family—and all three sons were reacting to one another with a sense of pride and joy and love. It was a moment made for a mother.

Now, watching J.R. swing from the living room to the kitchen Dorothy remarked on his sureness and confidence. "The way you move around here it would be hard for a stranger to tell that you were blind, J.R."

"Yes," he agreed, "I think I'm getting better all the time. You know, Mom, I started thinking about something last night. I think I'm ready to walk up the stairs."

Dorothy and Bob had been waiting for this decision. Neither had ever suggested it. They had hoped that the boy would self-start himself on that adventure. "Good idea," Dorothy said. "Then you'll be able to visit the kids and us upstairs. When do you want to do it?"

"When Dad's here."

The DeBolts expected the nineteen steps to be a greater challenge to J.R. than they had been to any of the others. J.R. had the added handicap of blindness which would keep him from studying the stair-climbing techniques of the other children on crutches. Bob described in detail the railing and balusters and the curve of the staircase and told J.R. how the other children hung their left arm over the railing and positioned the right crutch on the step above their feet. As best he could, he gave the boy a mental picture of the push-pull action that would hoist him to the next step.

J.R. listened intently, then a little impatiently. He gave no indication of fear or self-doubt.

"I think I understand," he said. He turned and felt for the railing and the step. In accordance with Bob's explanation he hooked his arm around the railing and placed his crutch on the next step. He paused for a moment, seeming to "psych" himself up for the trial, then grunted and lurched up to the next step. His left foot slipped and he started to fall backward, but Bob and Dorothy pushed him erect.

Their words of encouragement attracted the other children to the hall. Then J.R. pulled and heaved himself to the next step. Dorothy climbed alongside him while Bob was close behind. The boy began sweating. Dorothy had never before seen this look of determination and concentration on his face. He continued climbing. His foot sometimes slipped off a step, and he had to be pushed forward to regain his balance. Once,

Dorothy clutched him and could feel his heart pounding violently.

Occasionally J.R. paused to catch his breath, but he gave no hint of wanting to give up.

He knew he reached the top when he ran out of railing and he could feel no higher step with his crutch. His face was wet with sweat, and his hand shook from the effort and strain.

"Now I want to climb down the stairs," he said. It was tough. Several times he slipped and fell. Bob and Dorothy and Anh blocked his body from rolling down the staircase. J.R. laughed away each fall as Bob helped him to his feet. He continued to work his way down the stairs. When he reached the landing he slumped forward with fatigue, but he kept standing. The children gathered around him and called out congratulations. J.R. thanked them and said, "I never imagined that nineteen steps could be such a long, long way."

When J.R. was out of earshot, Sunee swung herself to Dorothy and said, "Mommy, I was surprised. I didn't think J.R. could do it. Not on the first time. It was so hard for me. I know it's even harder for him."

"I didn't think he'd make it, either, Sunee," said Dorothy, shaking her head. "J.R. fooled us."

After dinner that night J.R. remained at the table. Dorothy was removing dishes. J.R. said, "Boy, this has really been a big day, Mom."

Dorothy stopped clearing the table. "J.R., it's been fantastic. We're so proud. I can hardly wait to write to Blythedale. They didn't even believe you'd ever be able to walk on braces and crutches."

"I kind of felt that was what they thought."

"We came home and I said to Bob I bet you'd be able to climb stairs, and Bob agreed and said, 'Let's talk to God about it!' J.R., we talked to God, and God told us you could climb those stairs if you really wanted to. And you must have really wanted to, J.R., because you sure got up them tonight."

"You know what, Mom? Every time I think of those people who tell me I can't do something, I want to tell them, 'That's a dirty lie!' "

Dorothy felt her heart jump. This was the spunk, the gumption they'd been hoping to see come from J.R. Here was a boy willing and ready to deal with crushing disabilities. It took incredible courage to do what he did, but he had it. J.R. was going to be okay. He was going to make it.

J.R. agreed that for a time either Bob or Dorothy would accompany him on trips up and down the stairs. He needed someone with him in case of a fall. Unlike the other paralyzed children, he couldn't see where he fell. Unlike other blind people, he couldn't catch himself with his legs. But he would learn to fall—as the others had. And he would learn to navigate those stairs alone.

At about nine one night, some ten days after J.R.'s first climb, Dorothy and Bob were doing paperwork in their bedroom. A knock sounded on the door and Bob asked, "Who is it?"

"It's me, Dad," said J.R.

Bob felt a lump rise in his throat, and for a few moments he couldn't answer. He looked across his desk at Dorothy. She had closed her eyes and was holding her temples between her hands.

Bob cleared his throat and said, "Come on in, J.R."